The Swan Study Book

for Cello

by Cassia Harvey
based on The Swan, by Camille Saint-Saëns

CHP346

©2018 by C. Harvey Publications All Rights Reserved.

www.learnstrings.com
www.charveypublications.com

The Swan Study Book for Cello

Table of Contents

The Swan Exercises	**Page**
Part One (measures 1-5)	1
Part Two (meas. 6-9)	6
Part Three (meas. 10-17)	13
Part Four (meas. 8-28; end)	19

Additional Studies	**Page**
Tenor Clef Overview	25
Tone Overview	28
Preparatory and Technical Studies	34

Complete Piece	**Page**
The Swan	40

Notes

This book divides *The Swan*, by Camille Saint-Saëns, into short sections and provides exercises for mastering each section.

The exercises are written to benefit both the professional and the student.

Each exercise was written to teach a specific skill. **Shifts** are often repeated to help with acquiring muscle memory. **Double stops** are included for establishing relative pitch, building left-hand strength, and balancing the bow across two strings. Most of the bowing work focuses on the technique needed to produce a good **tone**.

Vibrato should be used throughout the book as soon as intonation is secure. Playing the exercises with vibrato will help balance the hand over the notes being played and will also help develop tone.

Occasionally, reminders to use vibrato are included over the notes. These are not exclusive to the notes they are referring to; vibrato should be used on as many notes as possible throughout the book.

©2018 C. Harvey Publications All Rights Reserved.

The Swan Study Book for Cello

Note: The Swan is broken up into sections in this study book. The complete piece is at the back of the book.

The Swan
Section One: Measures 1-5

The Swan, by Camille Saint-Saëns
Exercises by Cassia Harvey

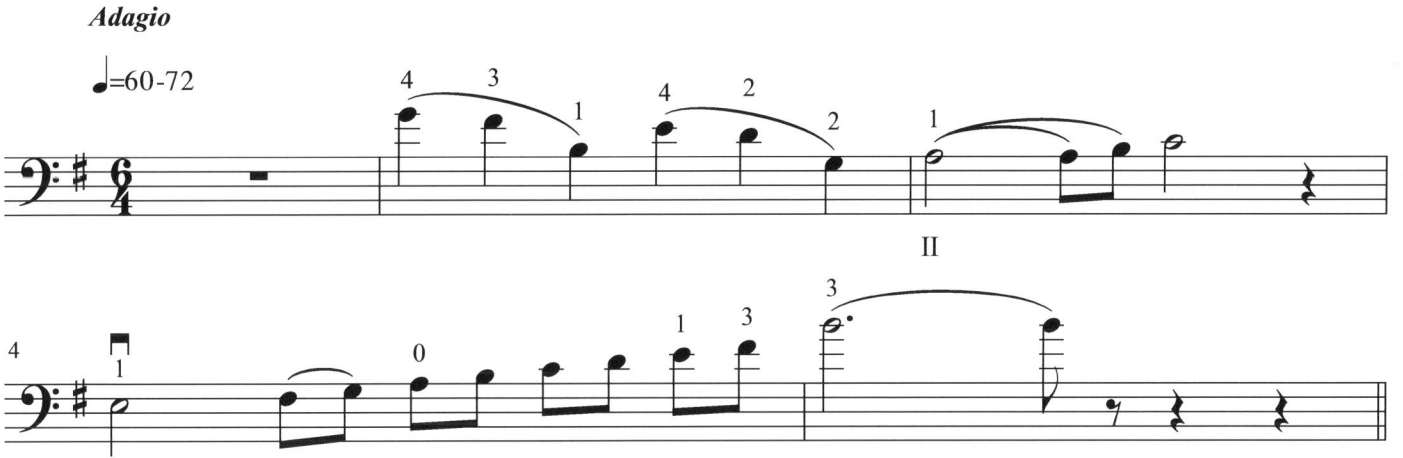

Learning the Notes and the First Shift
Measure 1

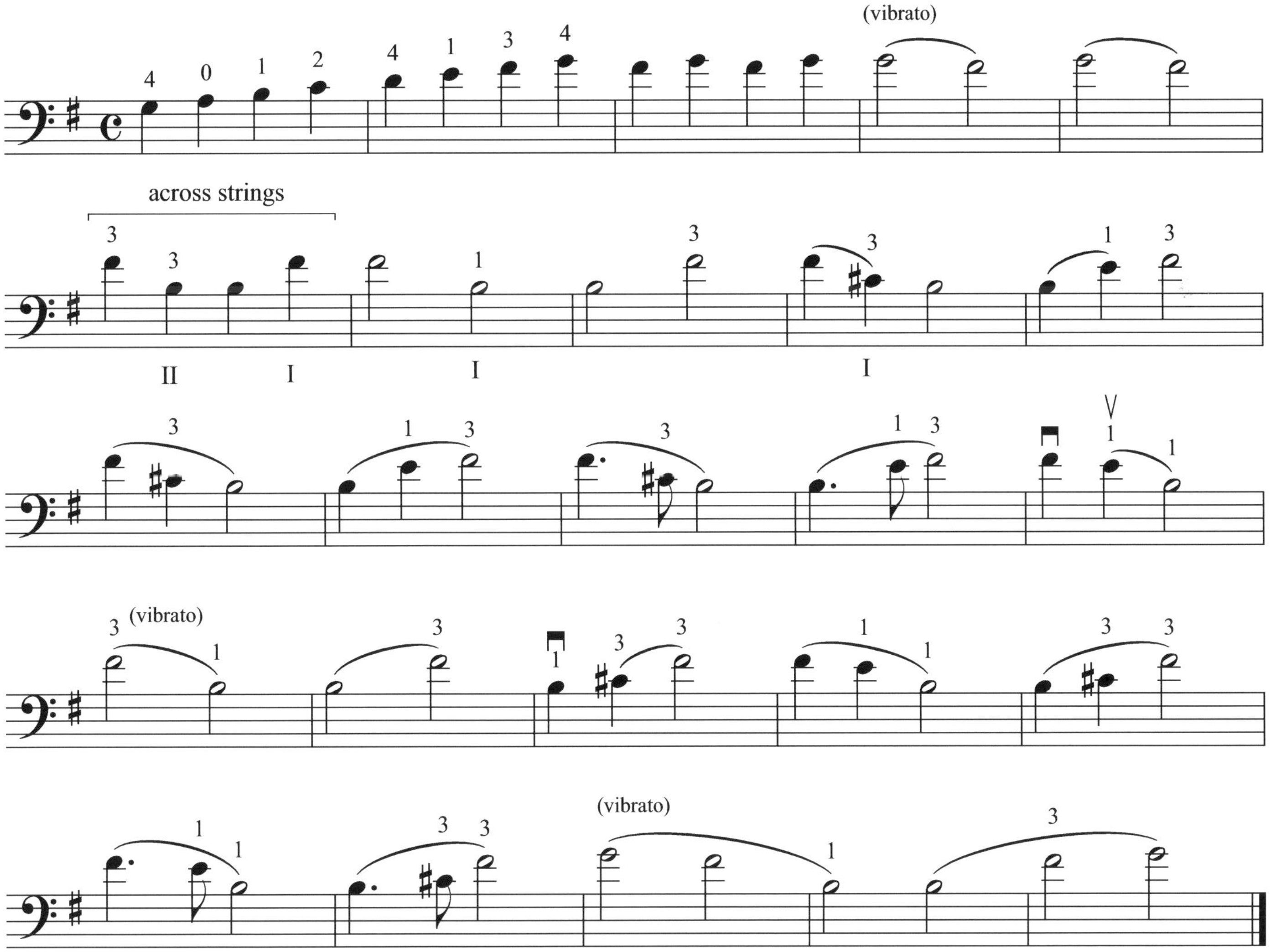

©2018 C. Harvey Publications All Rights Reserved.

The Second Shift
Measure 1

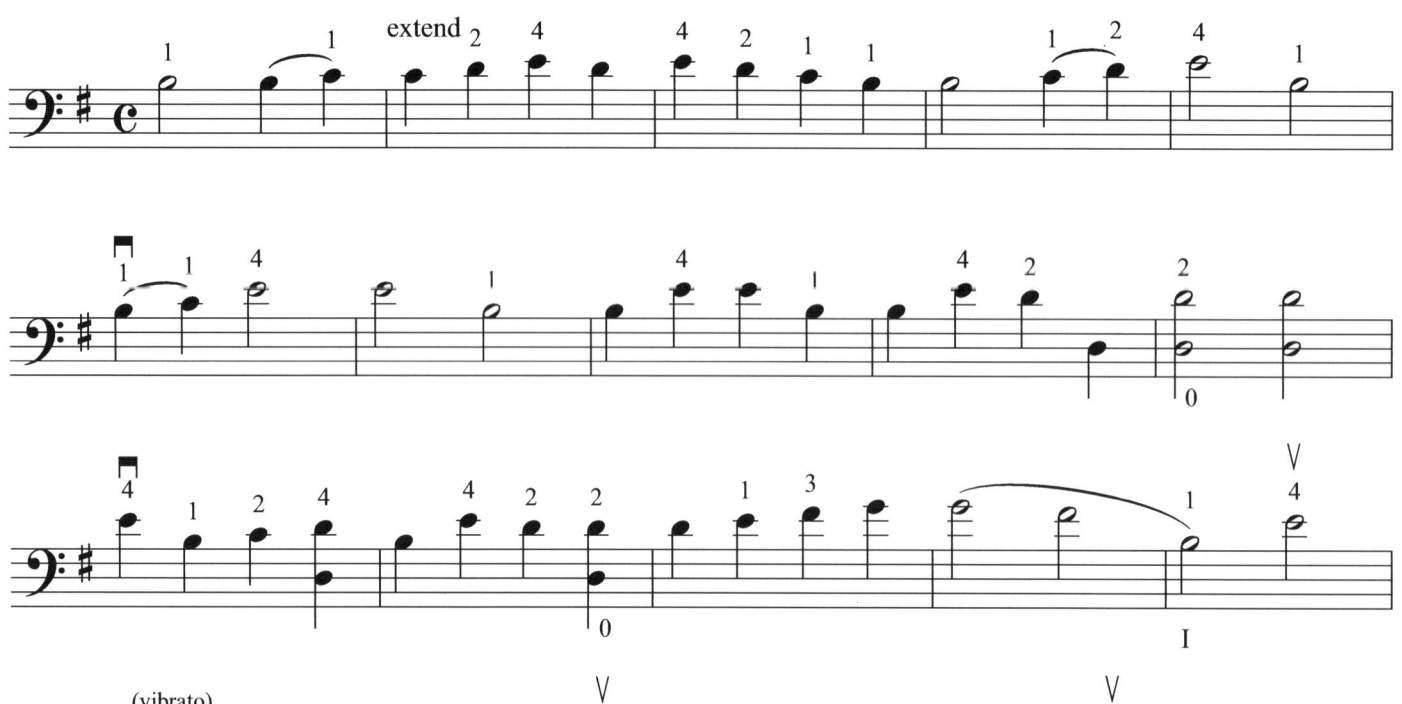

Playing Across Strings
Measure 1

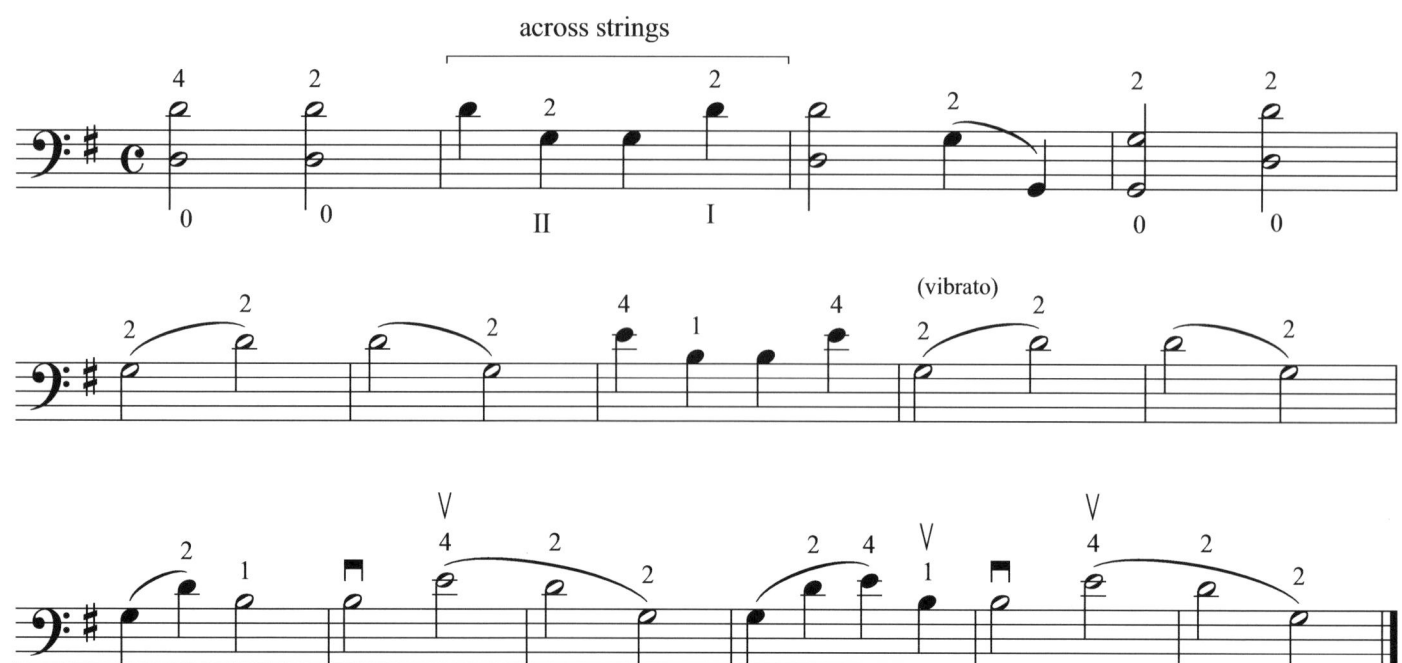

©2018 C. Harvey Publications All Rights Reserved.

The Swan Study Book for Cello

3

Bowing: Son Filé
Measure 1

Note: Start slightly faster and work to play this as slow as possible.

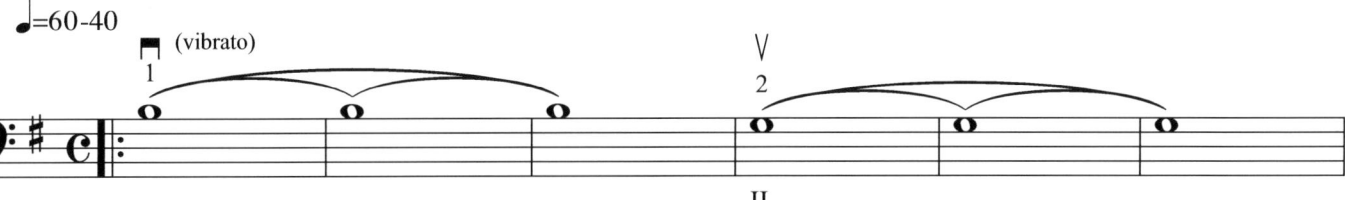

Bowing: String Crossing
Measures 1-2

Shifting to Fourth Position
Measures 1-2

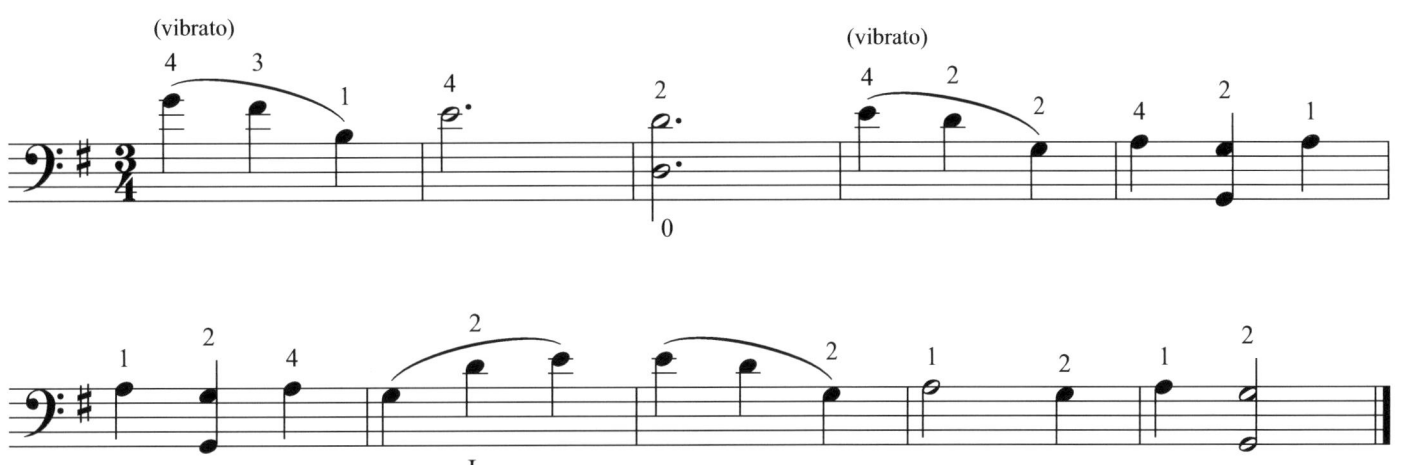

©2018 C. Harvey Publications All Rights Reserved.

Rhythm
Measure 2

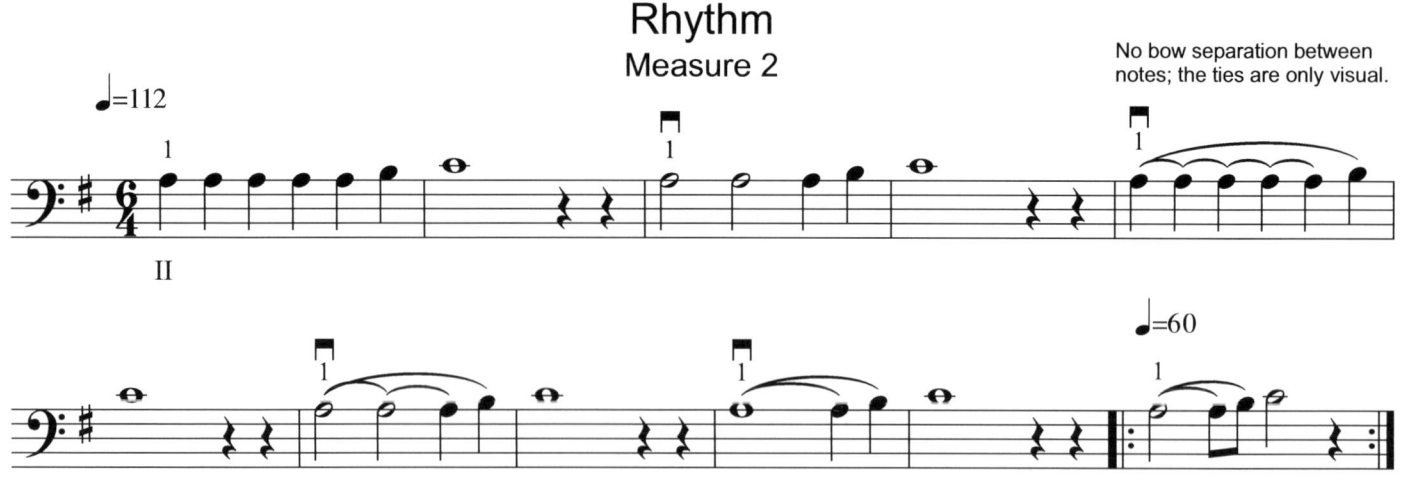

Double Stops for Intonation
Measure 1-2

Scales and Tone
Measure 3

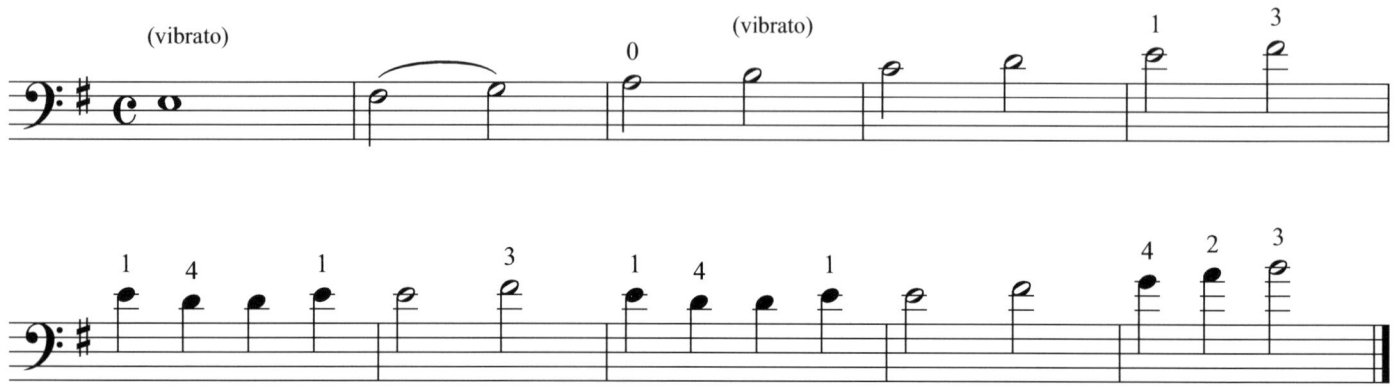

The Swan Study Book for Cello

Learning the Shift
Measures 3-4

Practicing the Shift I
Measures 3-4

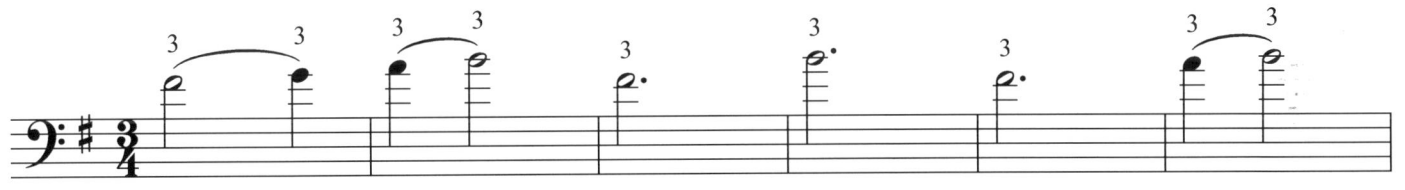

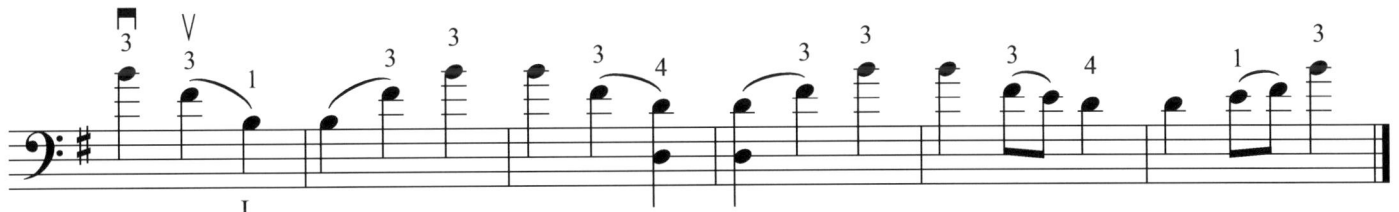

Practicing the Shift II
Measures 3-4

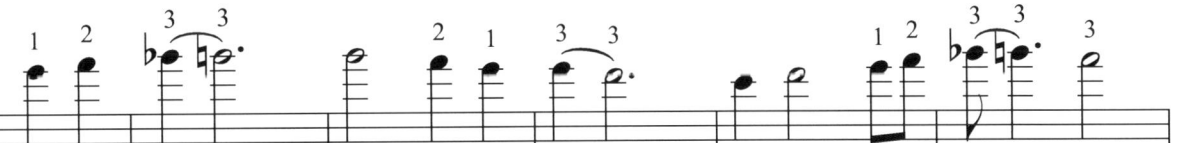

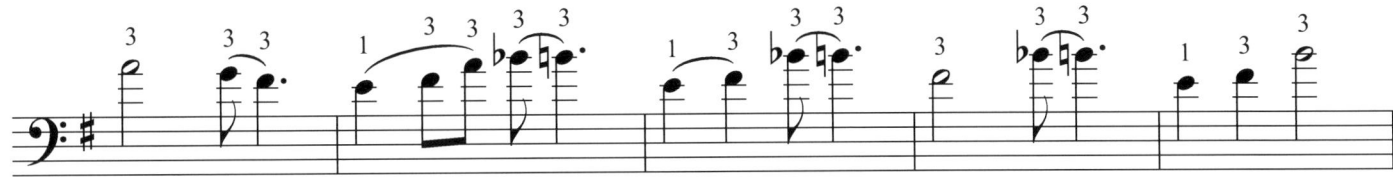

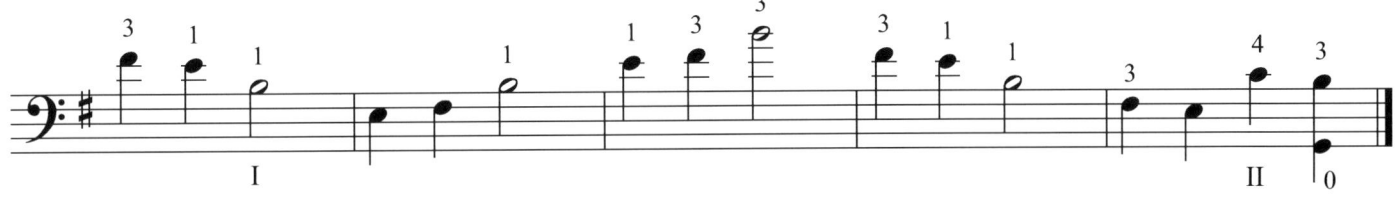

©2018 C. Harvey Publications All Rights Reserved.

The Swan
Section Two: Measures 6-9

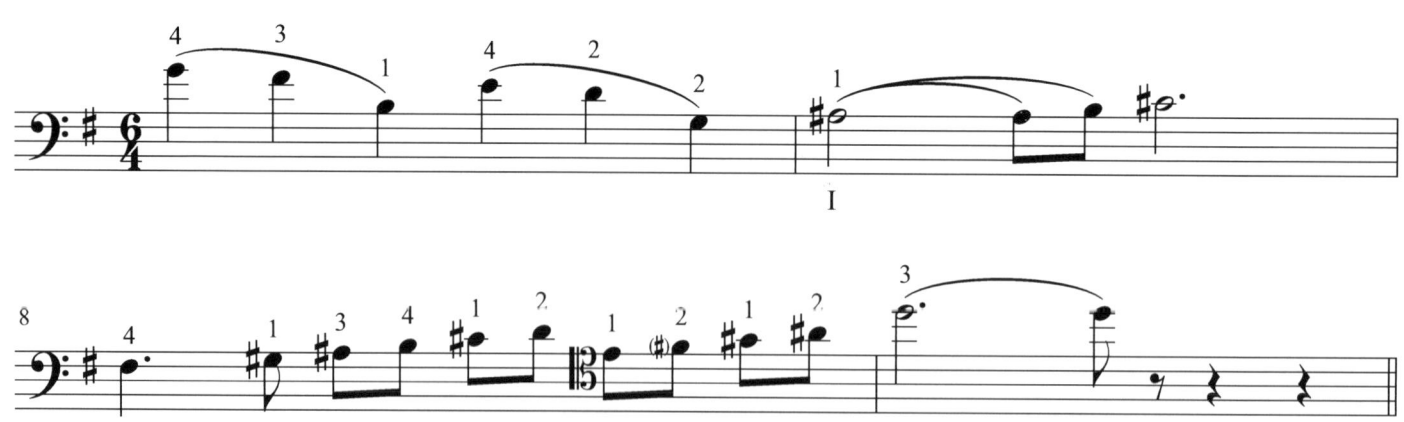

Bow Distribution Exercise III
Measures 6-7

Rhythm
Measure 7

The Swan Study Book for Cello   7

Shifting I
Measure 8

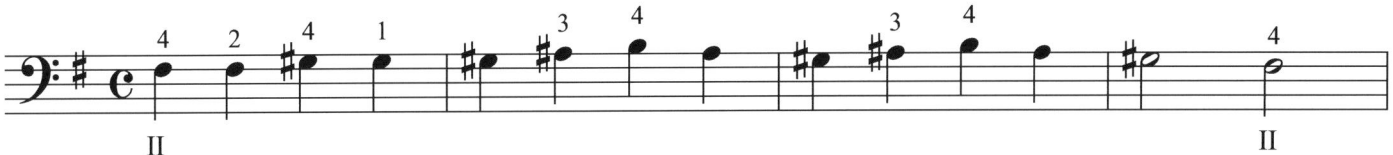

Shifting II
Measure 8

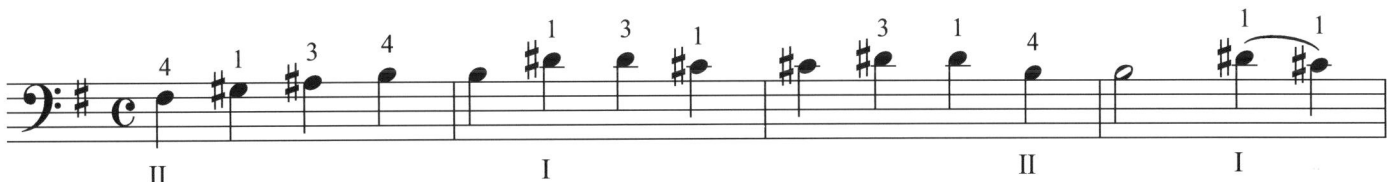

Shifting III
Measure 8

Note: To work on reading tenor clef, see page 25.

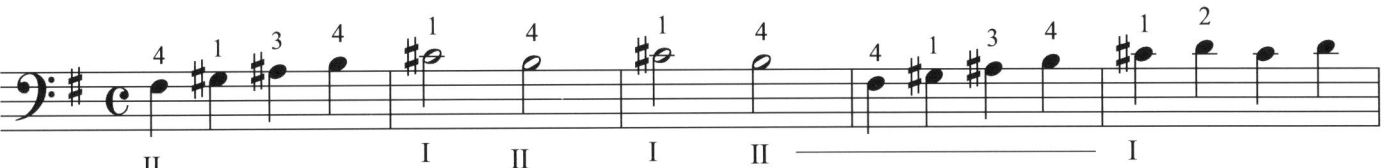

©2018 C. Harvey Publications All Rights Reserved.

Shifting IV
Measure 8

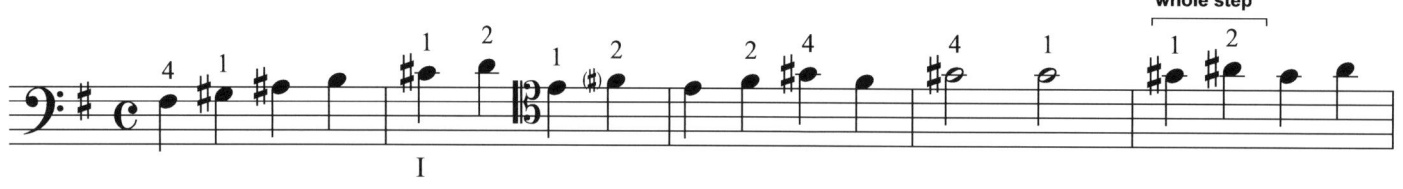

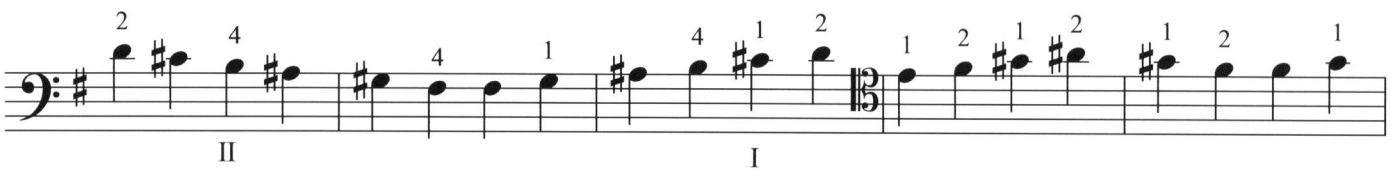
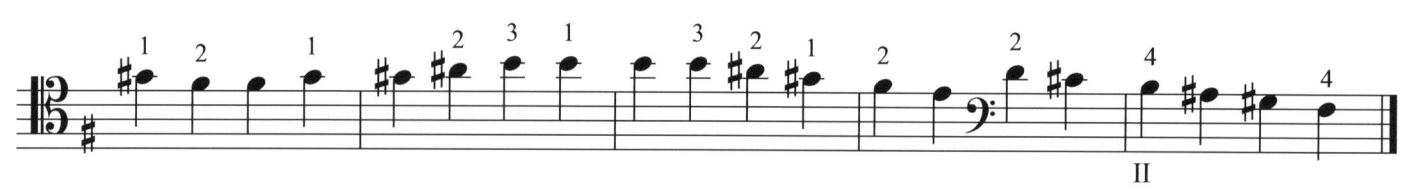

Shifting V
Measures 8-9

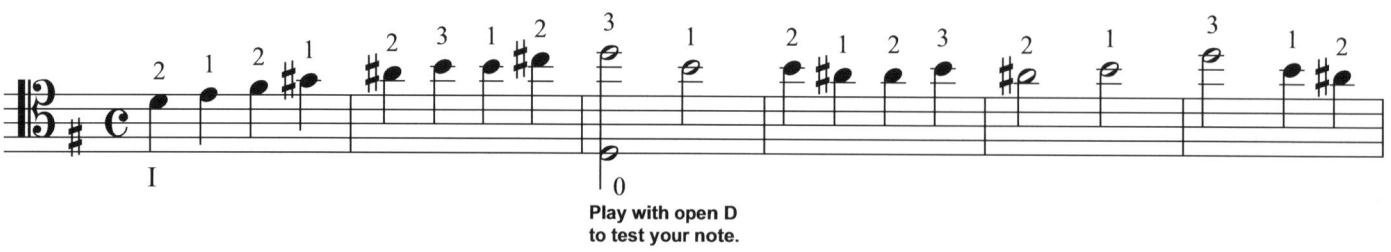

Play with open D to test your note.

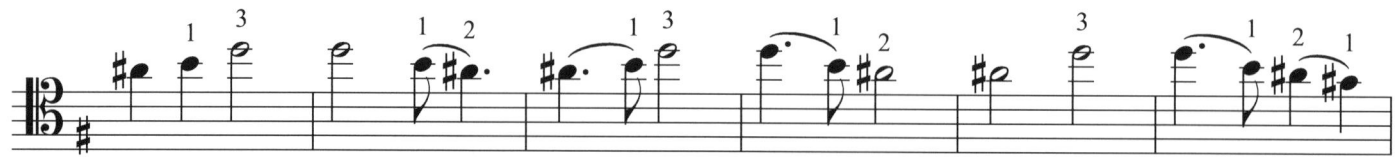

©2018 C. Harvey Publications All Rights Reserved.

The Swan Study Book for Cello

Shifting VI
Measures 8-9

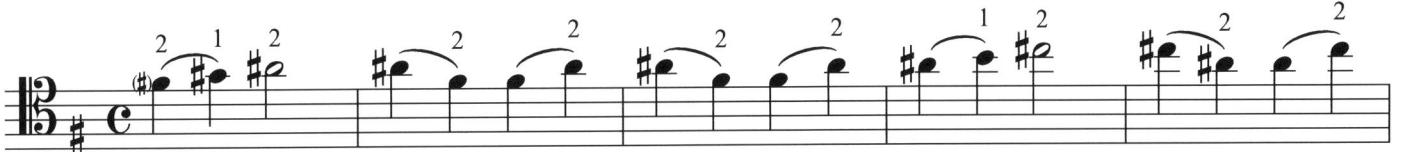

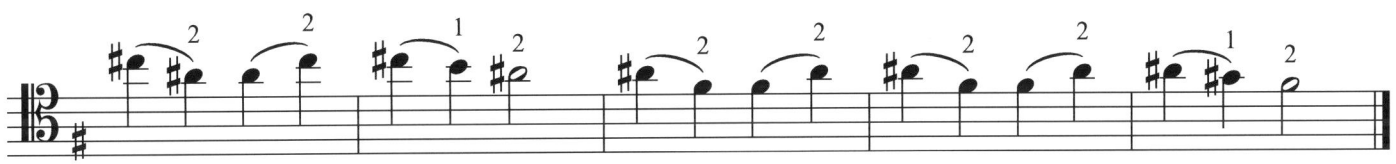

Using Grace Notes to Find the Top Note
Measures 8-9

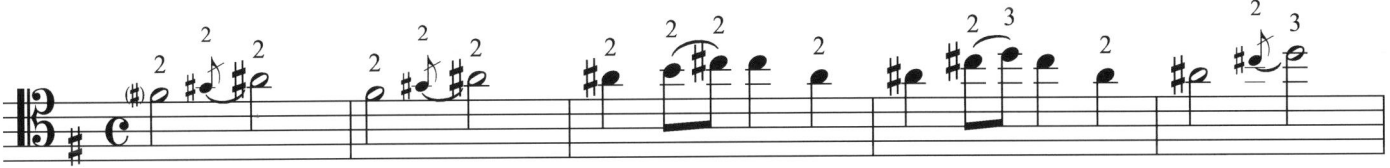

©2018 C. Harvey Publications All Rights Reserved.

Shifting Inside Slurs to Learn Distance (Optional Advanced Exercise)
Measures 8-9

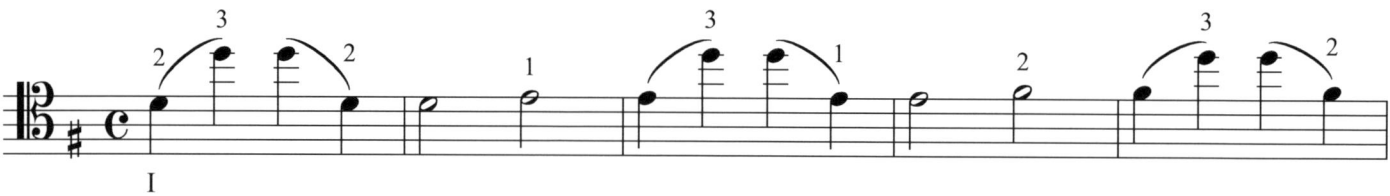

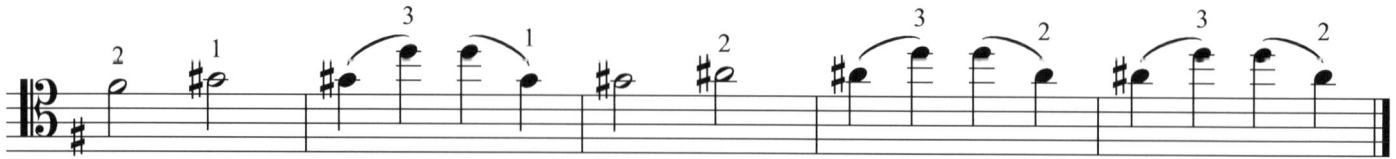

Shifting Patterns
Measures 8-9

Shifting in Rhythms to Prepare for Playing *The Swan*
Measures 4-5, 8-9

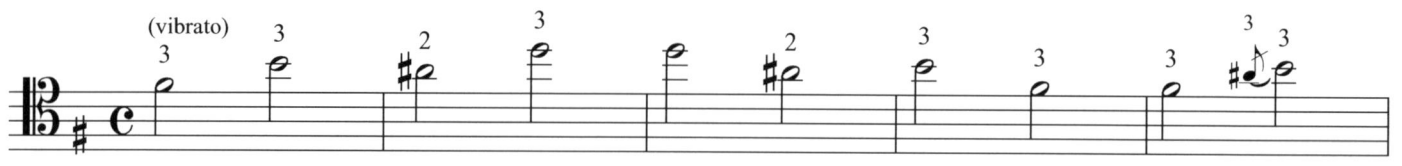

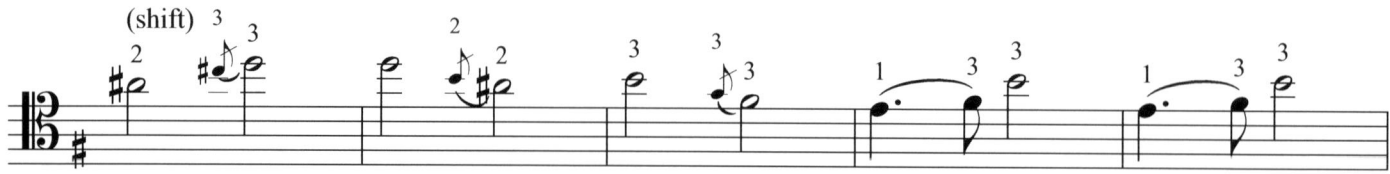

©2018 C. Harvey Publications All Rights Reserved.

Rhythm and Scales
Measures 8-9

Shifting and Tone
Measures 4-5, 8-9

For more work on tone, see Tone Overview on page 28.

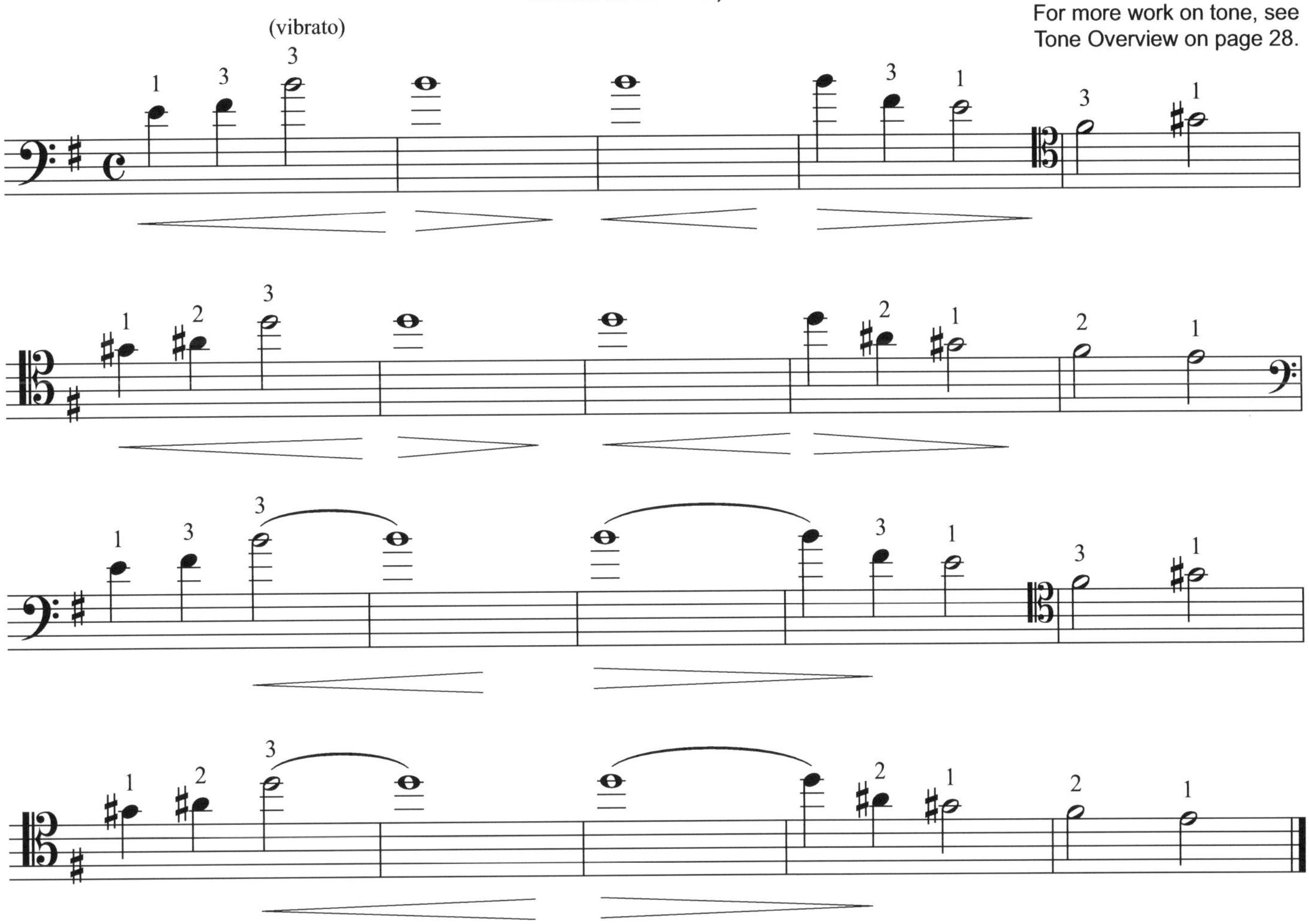

Finger and Bow Exercise
Measures 1-9

Double Stops for Intonation and Tone
Measures 8-9

The Swan
Section Three: Measures 10-17

Learning the Notes
Measure 10

Shifting Backwards I
Measures 10-11

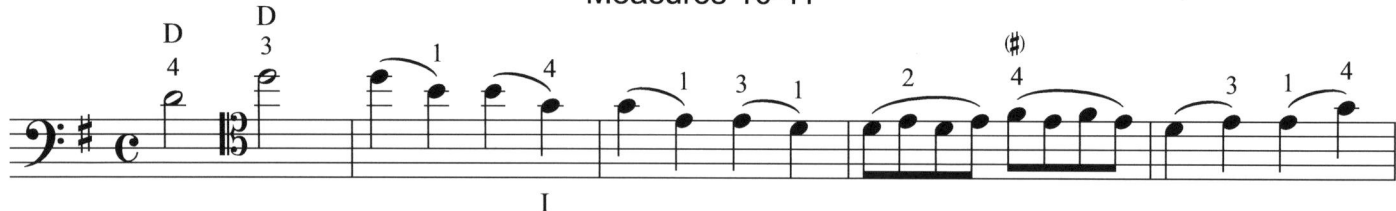

Shifting Backwards II
Measures 10-11

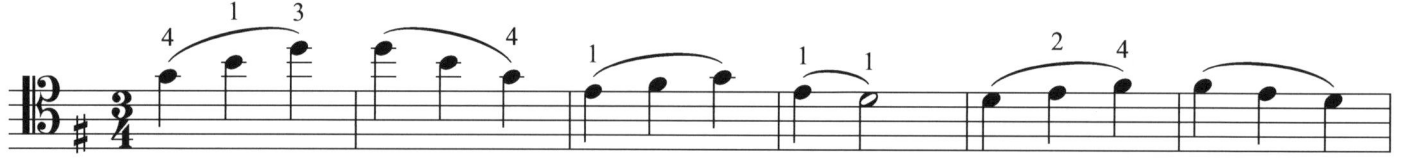

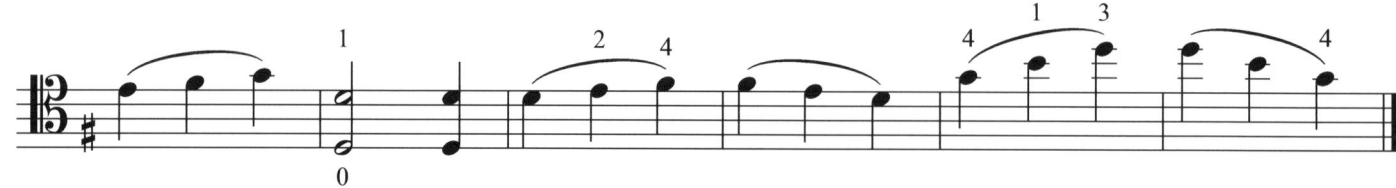

Shifting Backwards III
Measures 10-11

©2018 C. Harvey Publications All Rights Reserved.

Shifting Up to C♮
Measures 11-12

Shifting Back to F♮ and C♮
Measures 12-13

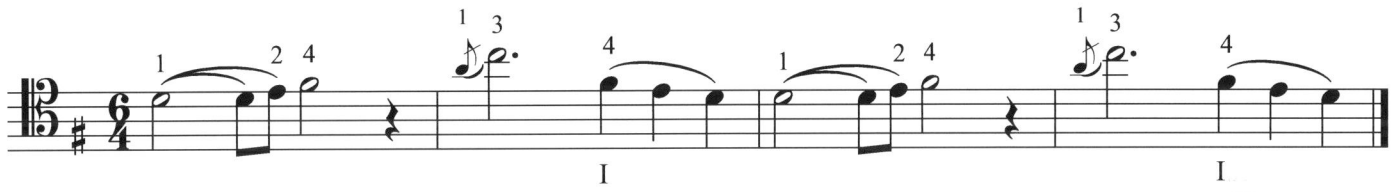

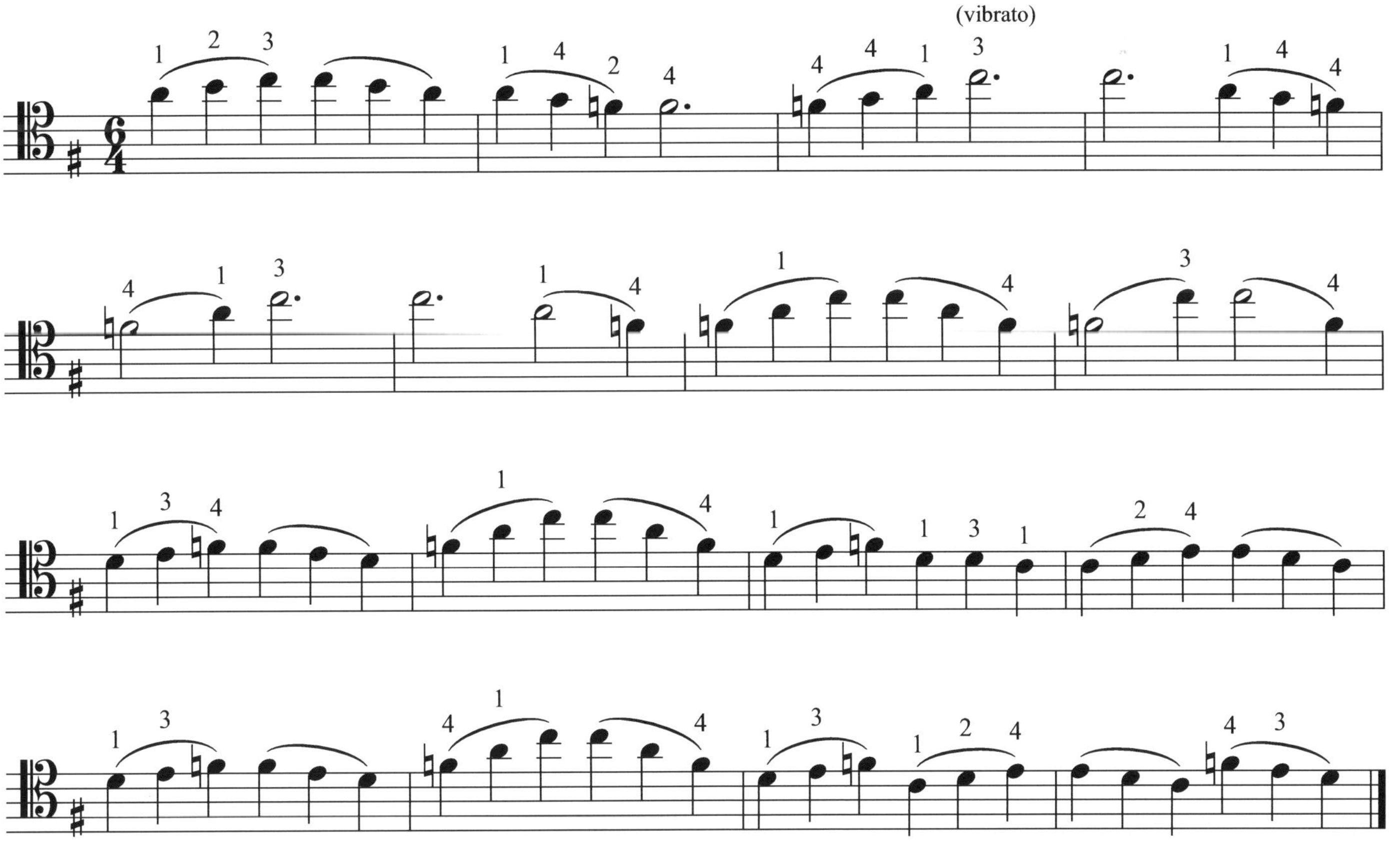

Mapping the Fingerboard I
Measures 10-13

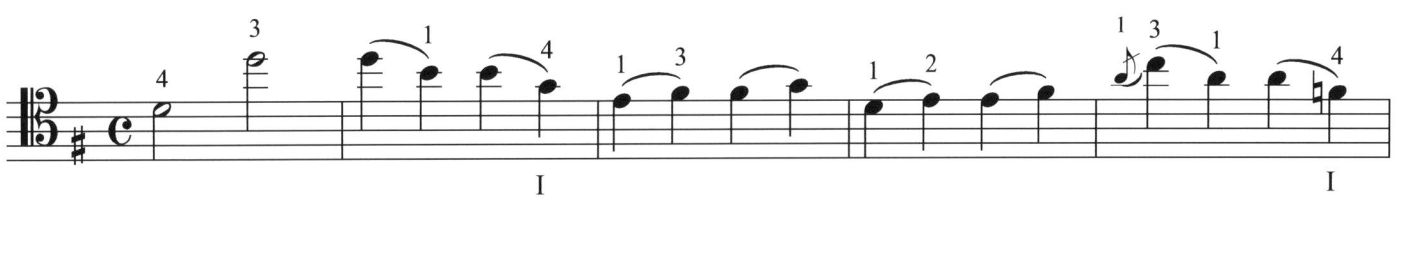
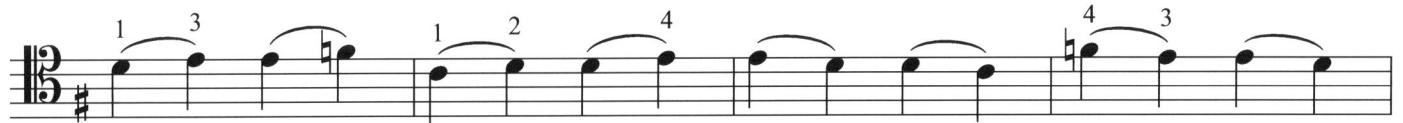
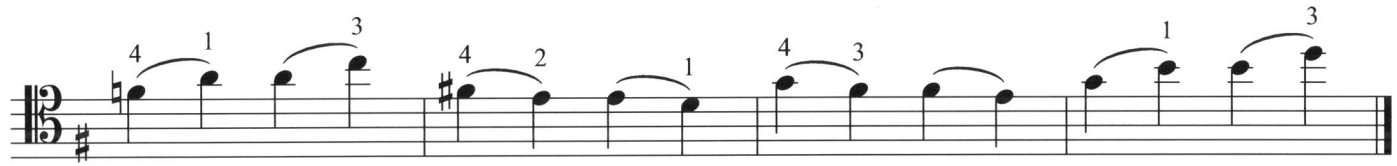

Mapping the Fingerboard II
Measures 10-13

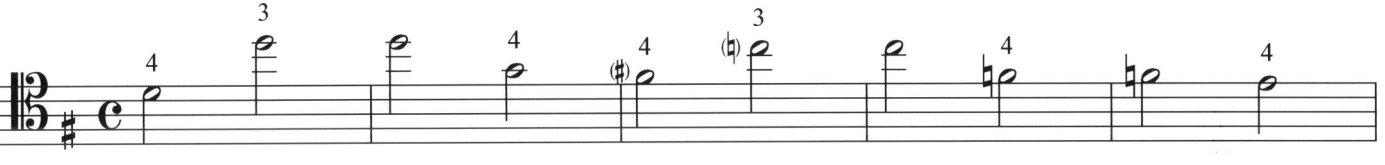
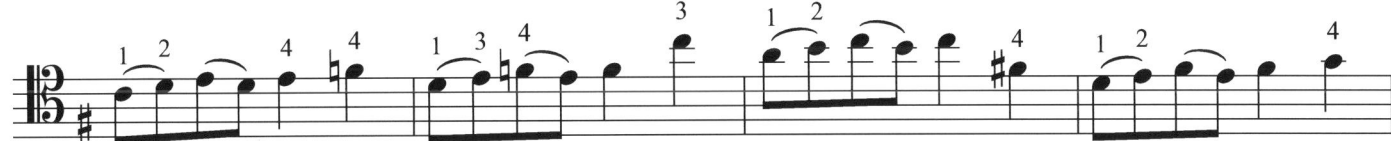

Learning the Notes I
Measures 14-17

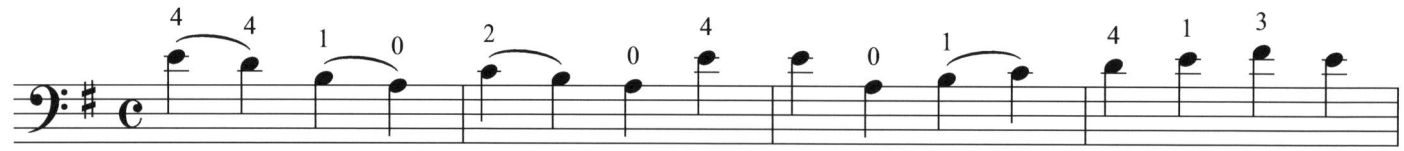

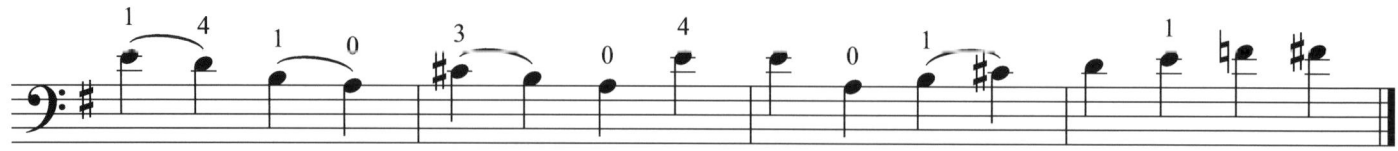

Learning the Notes II
Measures 14-17

Shifting
Measures 10-17

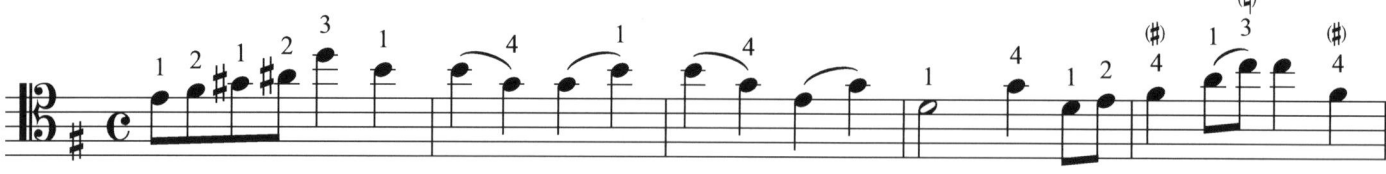

The Swan Study Book for Cello

The Swan
Section Four: Measures 18-28 (end), Bowing No. 1

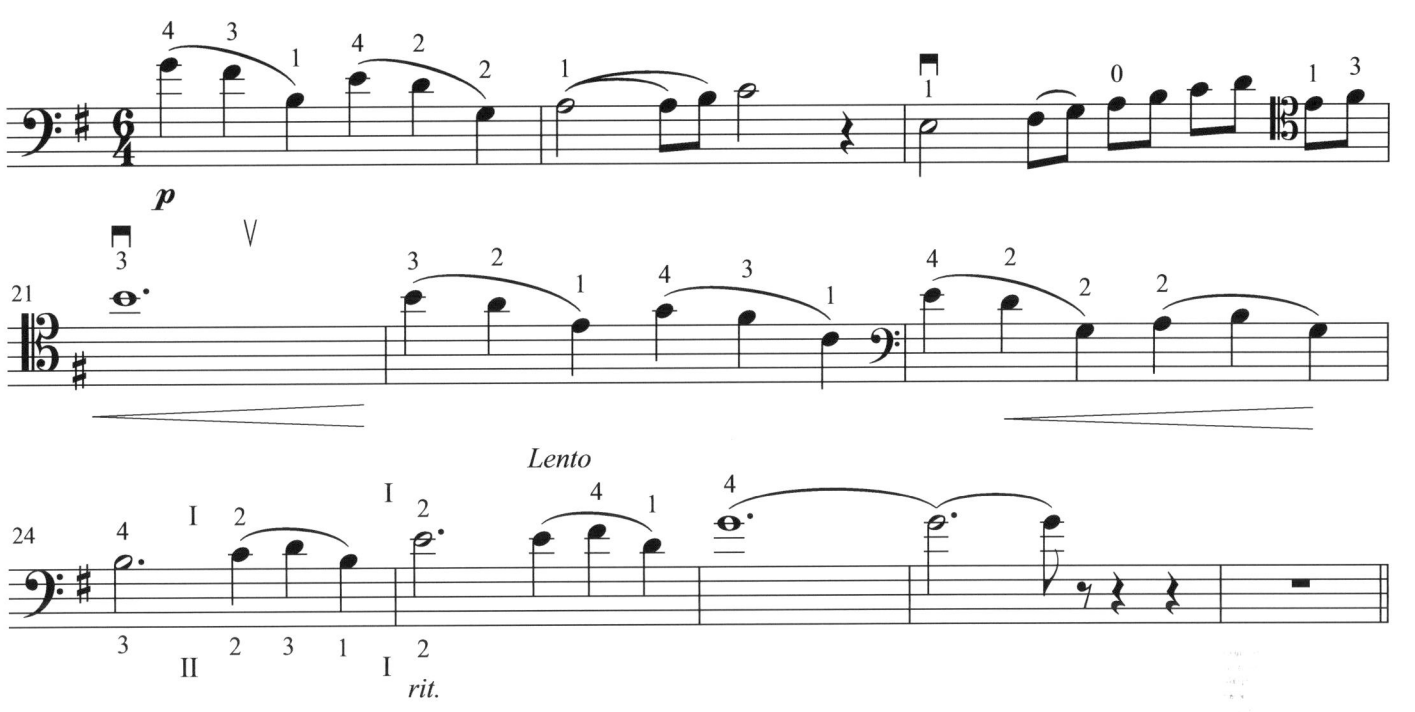

The Swan
Section Four: Measures 18-21, Bowing No. 2

Double Stops for Intonation
Measures 18-21

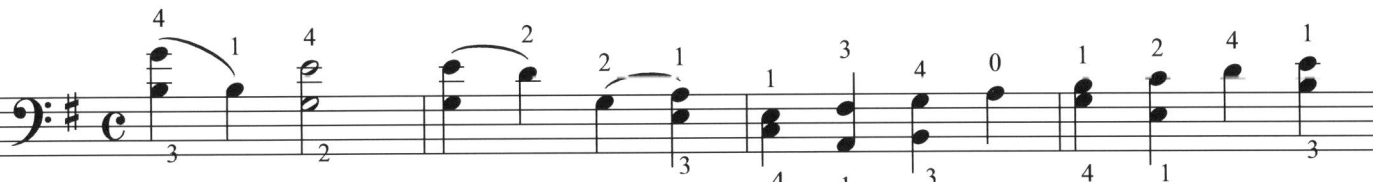

©2018 C. Harvey Publications All Rights Reserved.

Study for Bowing No. 1
Measures 20-21

Study for Bowing No. 2
Measures 20-21

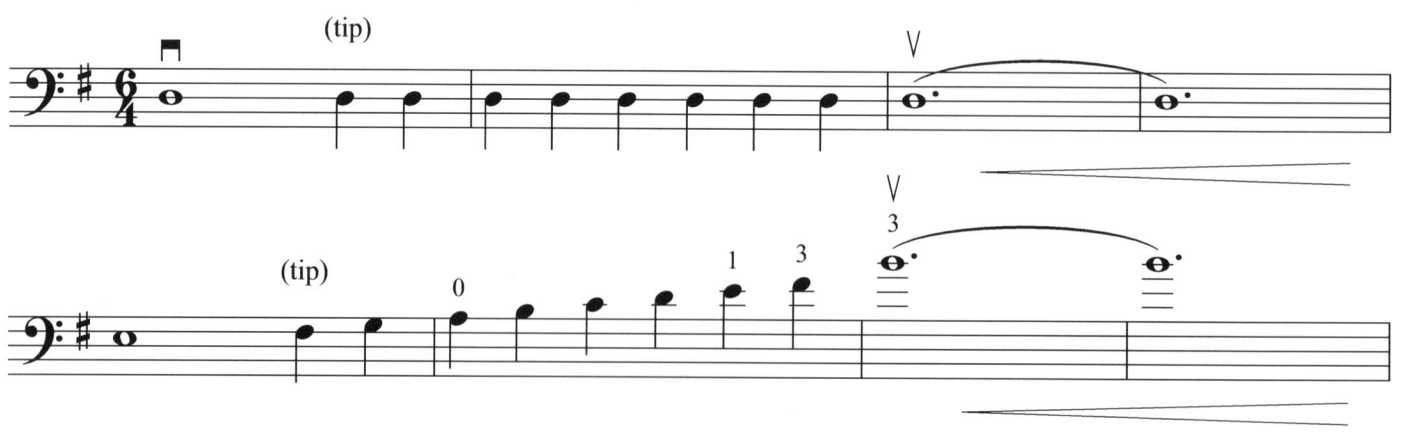

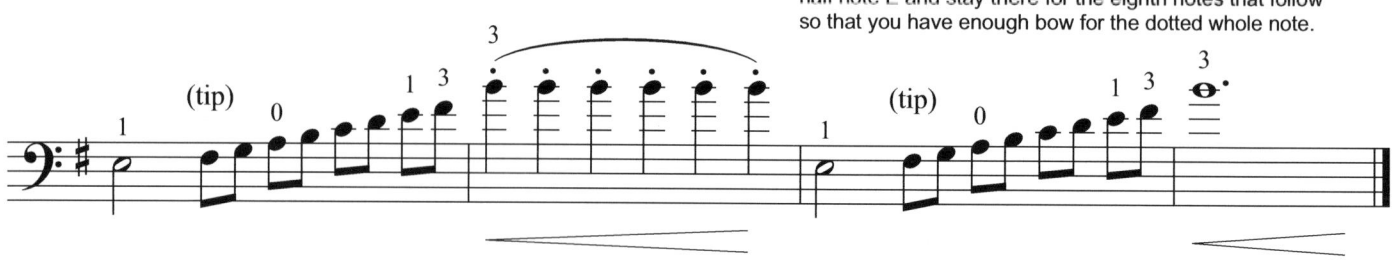

©2018 C. Harvey Publications All Rights Reserved.

Shifting Backwards III
Measures 22-23

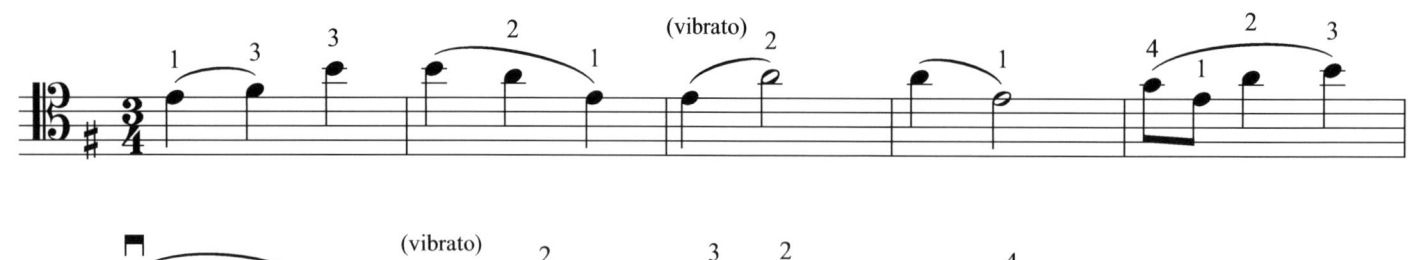
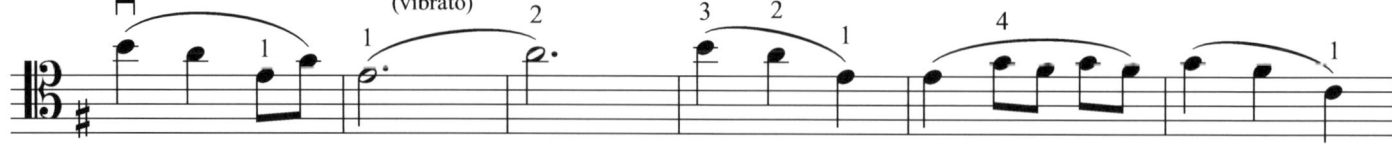
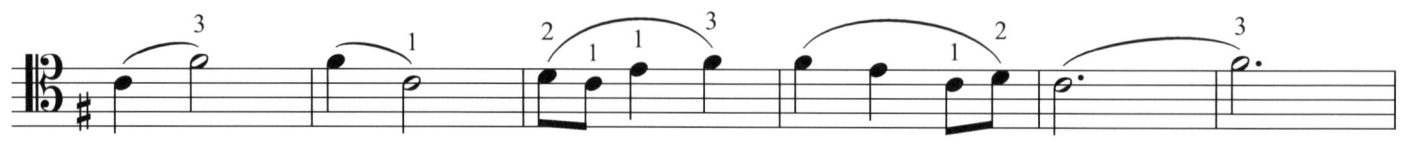

Shifting and Playing Across Strings
Measure 23

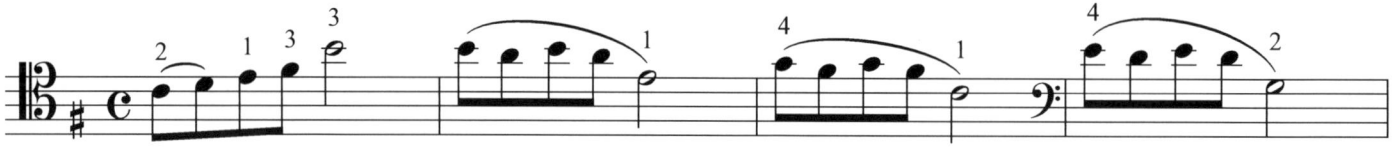
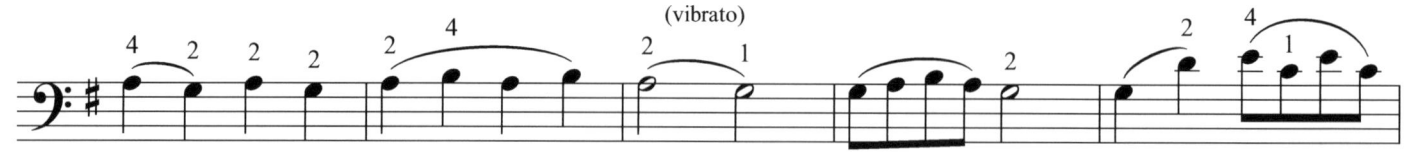

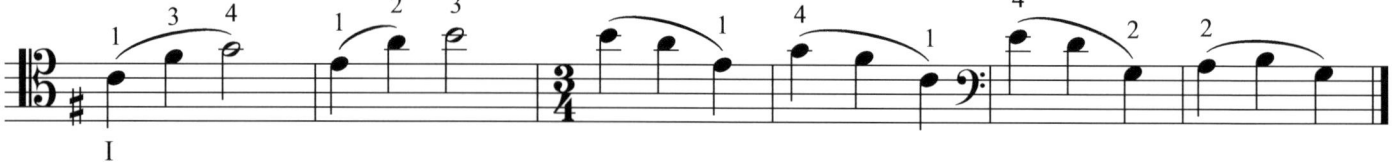

Shifting: Top Fingering
Measures 24-28

Balancing the Fingers for Vibrato: Top Fingering
Measures 24-28

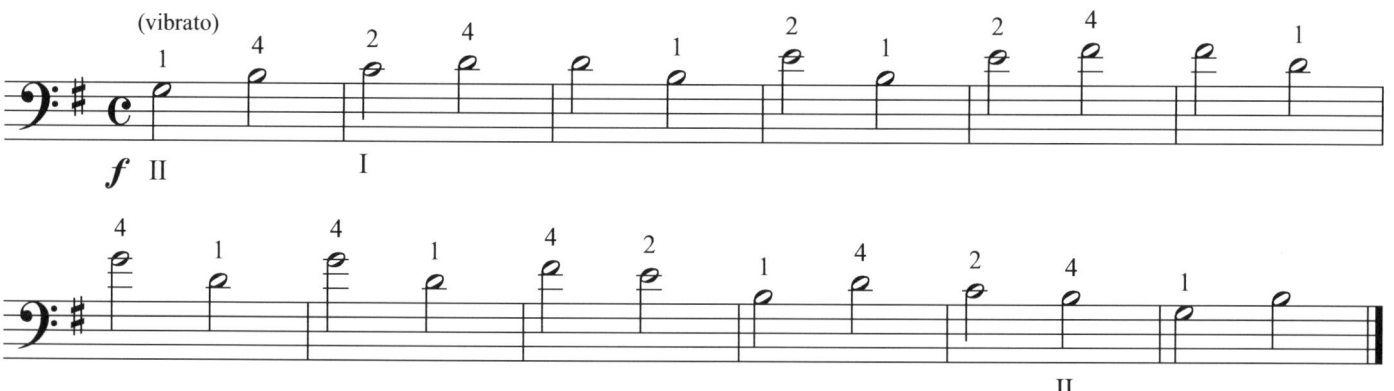

Learning the Notes: Bottom Fingering
Measure 24

Shifting and Tone: Bottom Fingering
Measures 24-28

The Swan Study Book for Cello

Tenor Clef Overview

25

Tenor clef can be used instead of bass clef to write notes for the cello.
Tenor clef is used to make high notes appear lower on the staff and avoid using unneccessary ledger lines.

The first time tenor clef is used in this edition of *The Swan* is in measure 8.

Measures 10-13

For more help learning tenor clef, you can use a method
such as *Tenor Clef for the Cello* (CHP109), from C. Harvey Publications.

©2018 C. Harvey Publications All Rights Reserved.

Measures 20-22

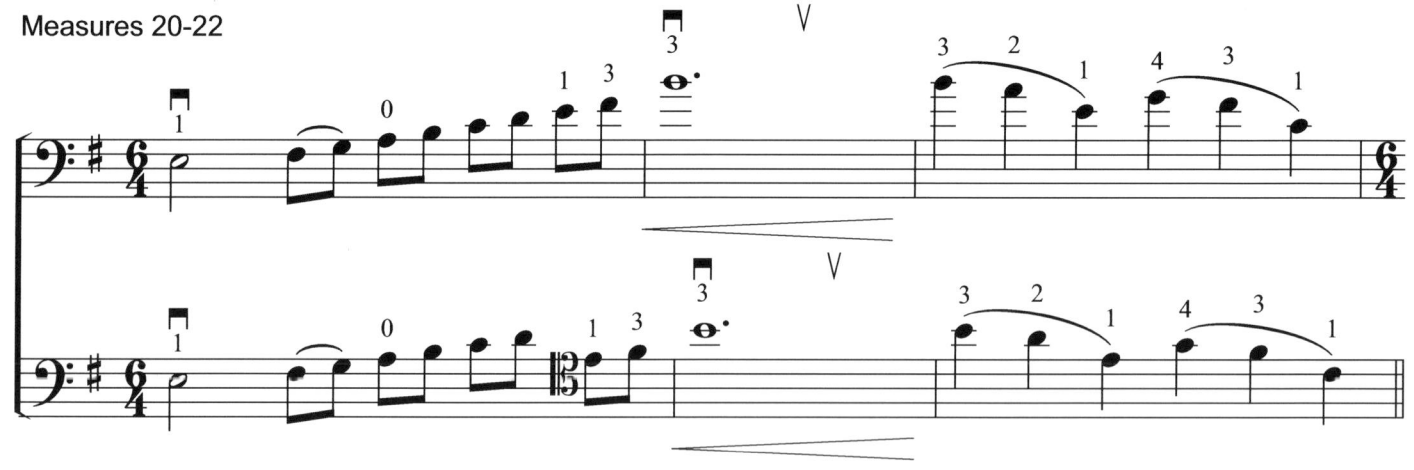

Note Chart

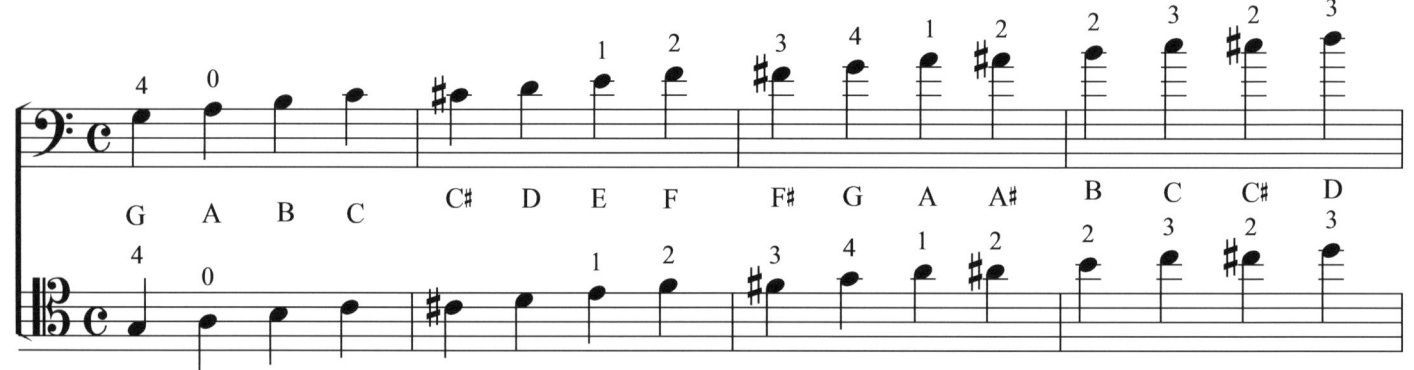

Tenor Clef Reading Exercise No. 1

The Swan Study Book for Cello

Tenor Clef Reading Exercise No. 2

Tenor Clef Reading Exercise No. 3

©2018 C. Harvey Publications All Rights Reserved.

Tone Overview

Good tone, or sound, comes from playing with good technique and listening to the effect that every motion has on your sound.

Tone is a product of both the left and right hands.

Here are some principles of good tone, along with exercises to work on each principle:

1. Stop the string completely with the fingers of the left hand.
To get better at stopping with strings with your fingers, use a combination of double stop exercises (to build hand strength) and finger agility exercises (to work on articulation and stop the string cleanly).

p Note: Play softly on these double stops so that you can listen carefully and see if both notes are pressed down all the way. If you hear a scratchy sound or an uneven sound, adjust your finger pressure to stop the string completely.

Repeat this exercise with loose vibrato on the double stops, if possible. Taking your thumb off of the cello neck can help.

Note: Make sure your fingers are curved and that you are playing on the fingertips. Balance your fingers over both strings and make sure your fingers hit the string cleanly and make a clear sound.

©2018 C. Harvey Publications All Rights Reserved.

2. Play at the correct soundpoint. Imagine 5 lanes, called soundpoints, between the fingerboard and the bridge. Soundpoint #1 is where you should play fast separate bows. As the bow pressure increases, move closer to the bridge (towards Soundpoints #2-5.) As the bow speed decreases, move closer to the bridge (towards Soundpoints #2-5.) And as the notes go higher (higher positions), move closer to the bridge (towards Soundpoints #2-5.) *The Swan* would be played mostly at Soundpoints #2-4.

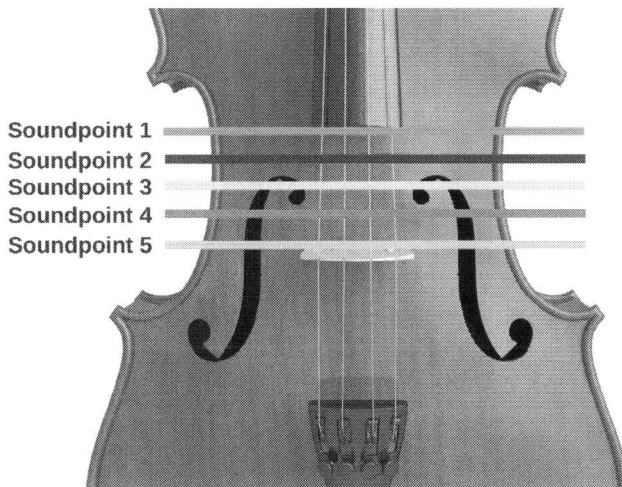

In these exercises, play each measure at the soundpoint listed under the measure. To get from one soundpoint to another, gradually move up or down as the bow is moving across the strings.

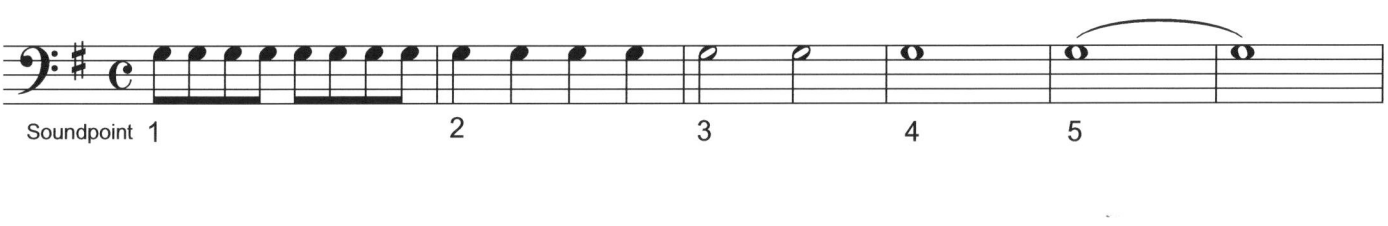

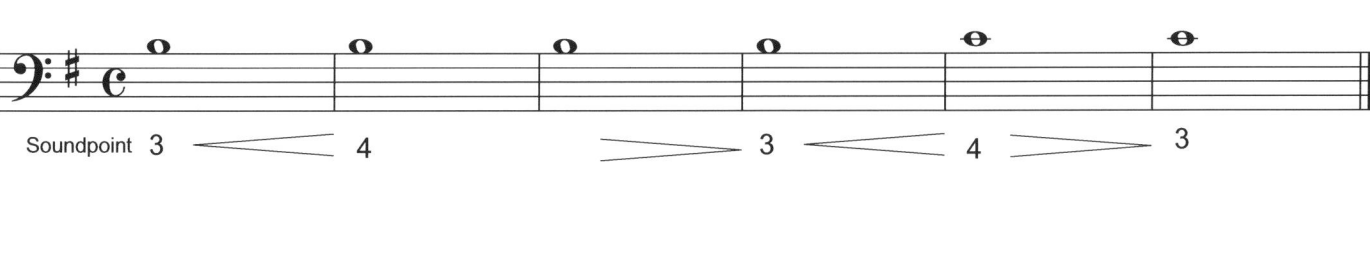

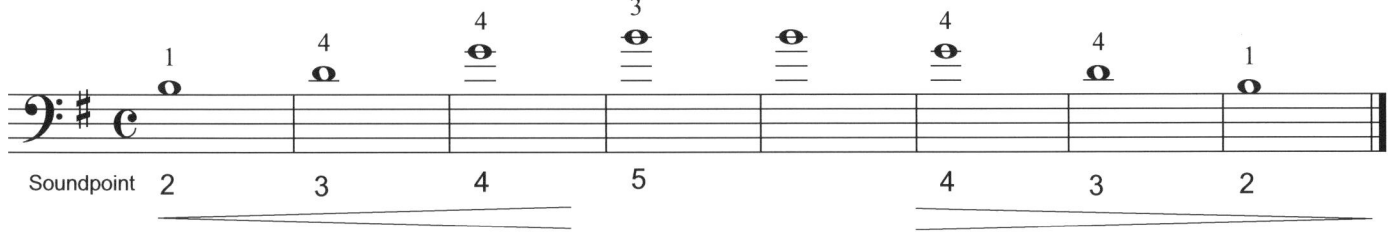

3. Good tone comes from choosing the best combination of bow speed, bow pressure and soundpoint. Practice increasing pressure and decreasing bow speed; this will make a harsh, scratchy sound. Then practice increasing pressure and increasing bow speed; this can make the sound cleaner. The third variable that affects bow speed is soundpoint (see No. 2 on page 29). When you have worked on the exercise below and varied your bow speed and pressure, try the same notes at different soundpoints.

Tip: Don't forget to play with a straight bow. Practicing next to and in front of a mirror can help with this.

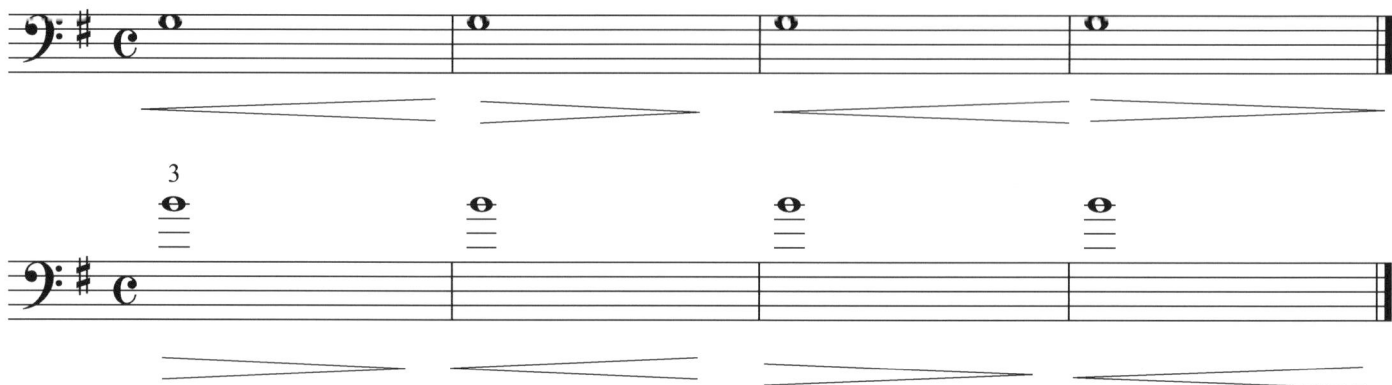

4. Catch the string with the bow. If you don't catch (grab) the string at the start of a bow, the hair will slide over the string without causing the string to vibrate. In the exercise below, staccato is used to help you practice catching the string. On the last line, start the bows cleanly but without an obvious "catch" sound.

©2018 C. Harvey Publications All Rights Reserved.

The Swan Study Book for Cello

5. Vibrato can help you make your dynamics more effective. As you crescendo, make your vibrato slightly narrower and more rapid. As you decrescendo, relax the vibrato into a slightly wider and slower motion.

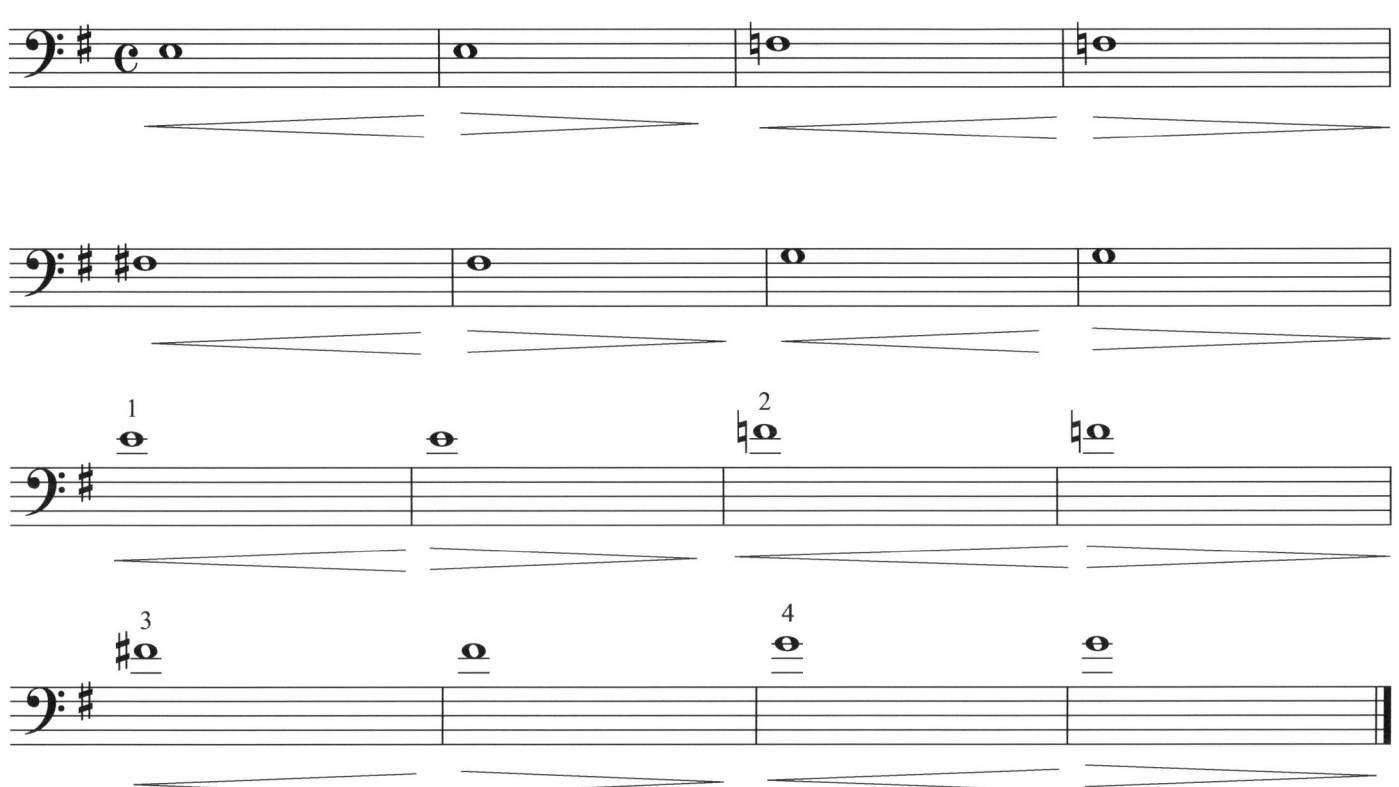

6. Listen! Without judging yourself harshly, simply listen for the effect that each motion has on the sound. If your bow moves faster or slower, if it plays closer to the bridge, if you aren't stopping the string completely with your left-hand fingers, or if the bow is not straight, the sound will be affected. Simply listening for the sound that is produced by each of these variables can help you decide what needs to be fixed in order to improve your tone.

Try this Son Filé exercise with your eyes closed to listen to your sound and adjust your technique to create the most beautiful tone possible. Start at ♩=60 and repeat, gradually getting slower until you get to ♩=40.

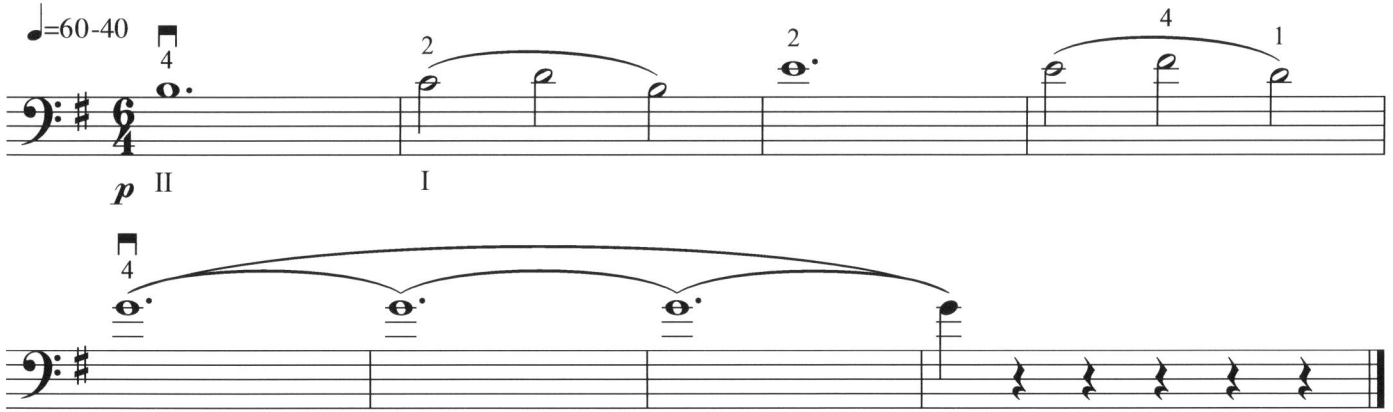

©2018 C. Harvey Publications All Rights Reserved.

Portamento

A portamento is a slide from one note to another.
A portamento is often used to make notes more expressive.
While a cleaner sound and less portamento is favored in current playing styles, more portamento was used in the past and we can expect that Saint-Saëns probably heard The Swan played with quite a bit of sliding.

Used sparingly, the portamento can be an effective tool in expressive playing. Avoid sliding down to a note and then immediately back up again; usually a slide in one direction is enough.

To use portamento, relax your fingers as you slide and slide a little slower than usual, allowing the sound of the slide to be heard.

A portamento may be indicated by a line:
However, most of the time, it is not notated and simply used by the individual musician when it seems appropriate.

For an effective portamento, slide on the arrival finger (the finger of the note you are sliding *to*.)

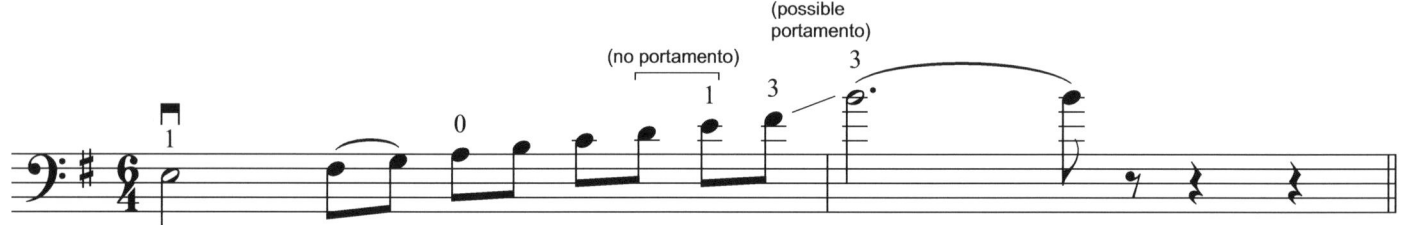

Rubato

Rubato: robbing time. "Steal" time from one group of notes and give it to another to make the music more expressive.

Rubato, when used sparingly, can be an effective tool in highlighting the parts of the music that you find more important. Holding one or more notes slightly longer than other notes can make them stand out to the audience. Playing *The Swan* with rubato is standard, however keep in mind that the accompaniment is a constant sixteenth note rhythmic pattern. Using too much rubato will make you difficult to follow as a performer.

Bow Distribution (Not Running Out of Bow)

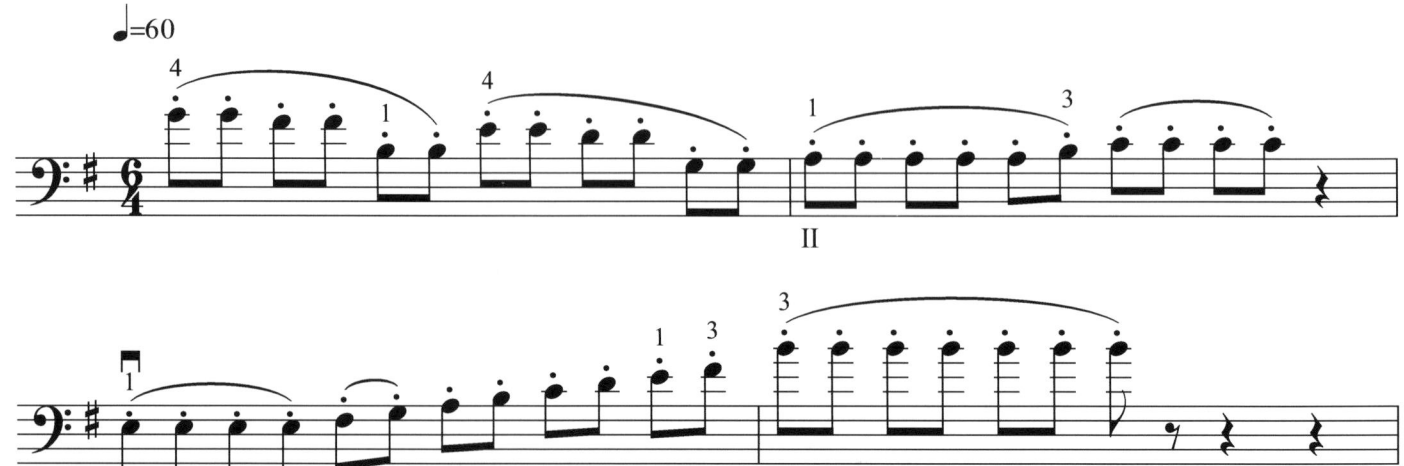

©2018 C. Harvey Publications All Rights Reserved.

Preparatory and Technical Studies

G Major Scale Fingerings to Prepare for *The Swan*

Positions

Roman numerals refer to strings:
I = A string
II = D string
III = G string
IV = C string

Fourth Position

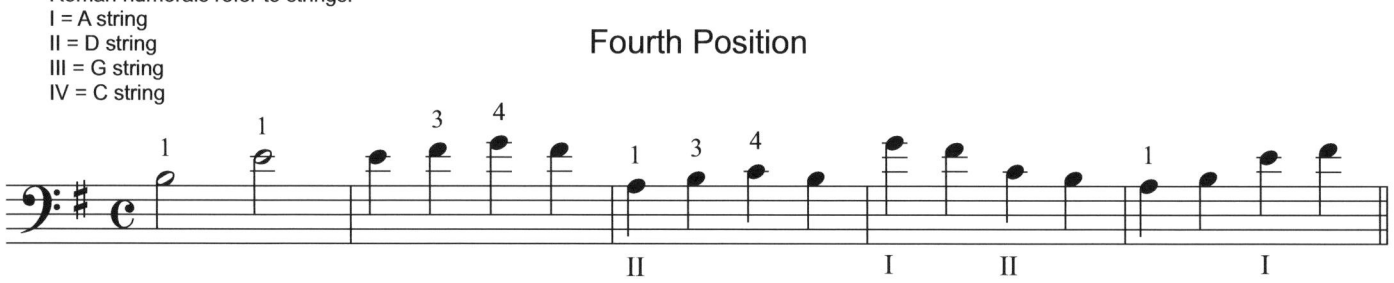

Third Position

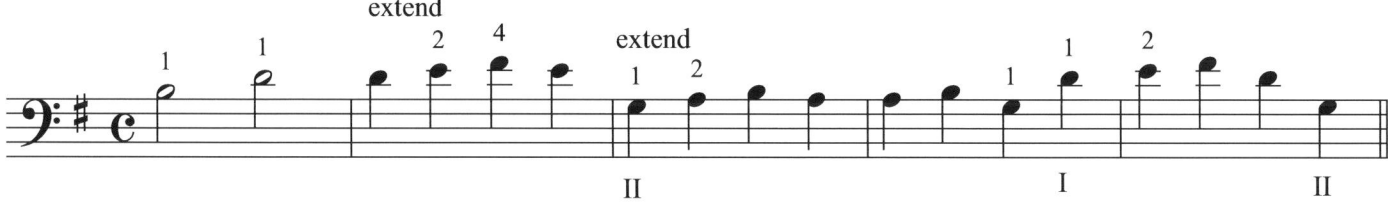

Second Position

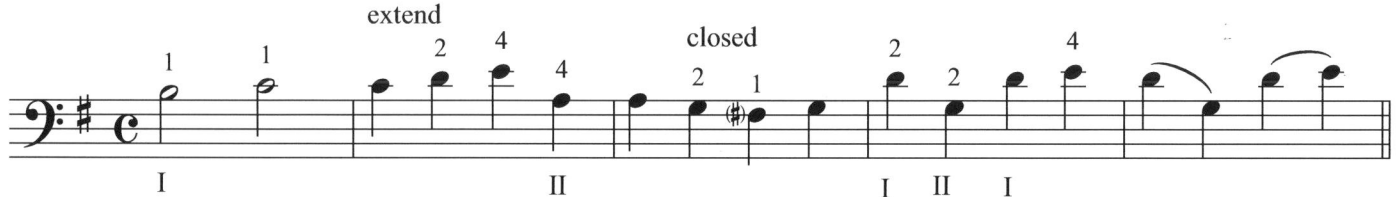

Half Position

Shifting Exercise

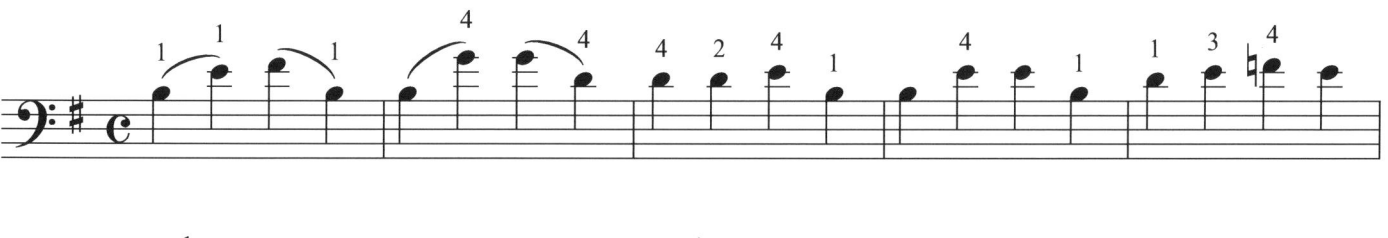

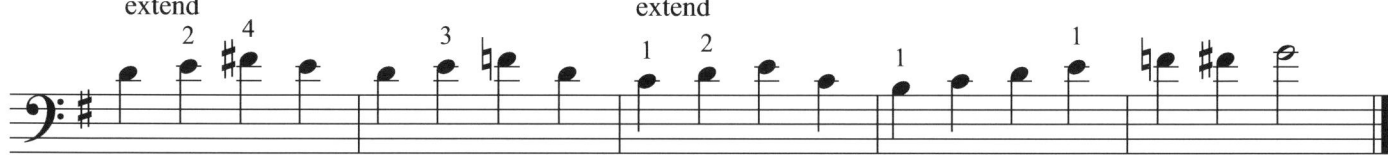

36

Little Scales

Shifting Patterns

The Swan Study Book for Cello

Octave Shift: B to B

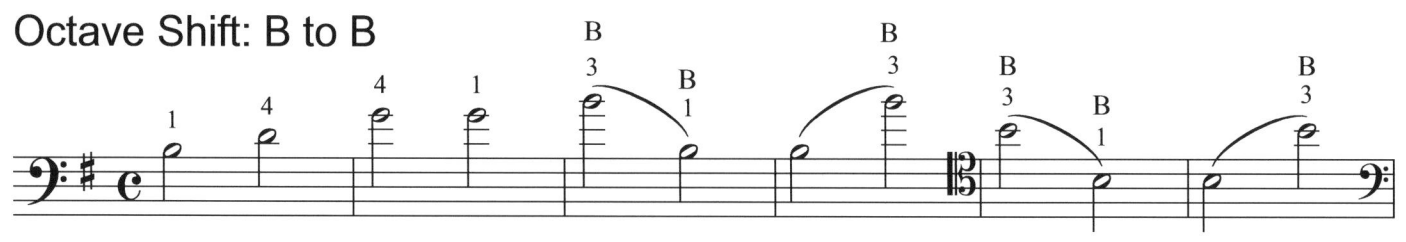
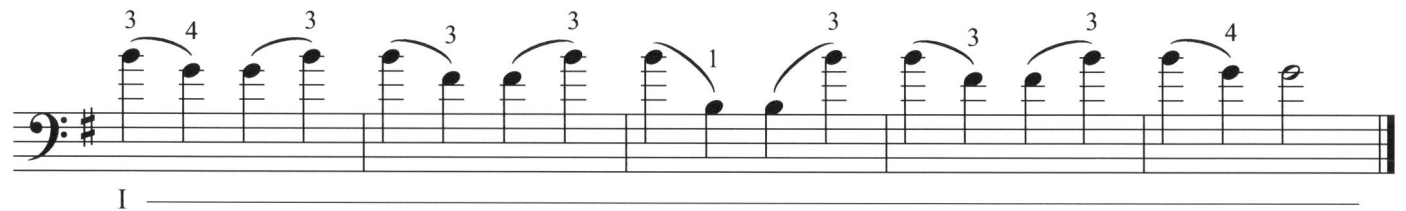

Octave Shift: C to C

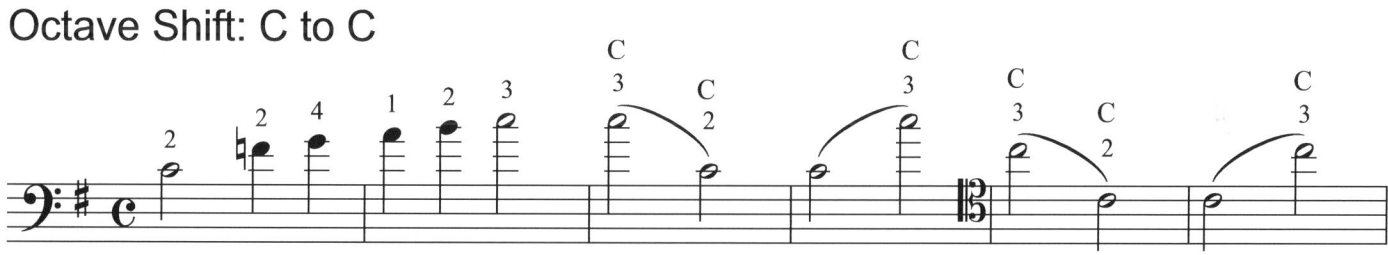
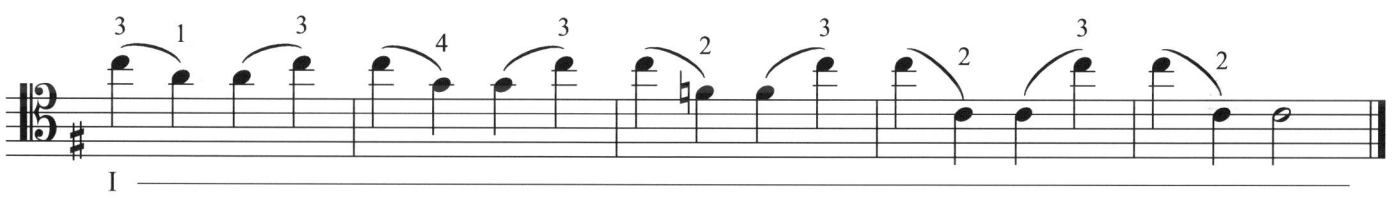

Octave Shift: D to D

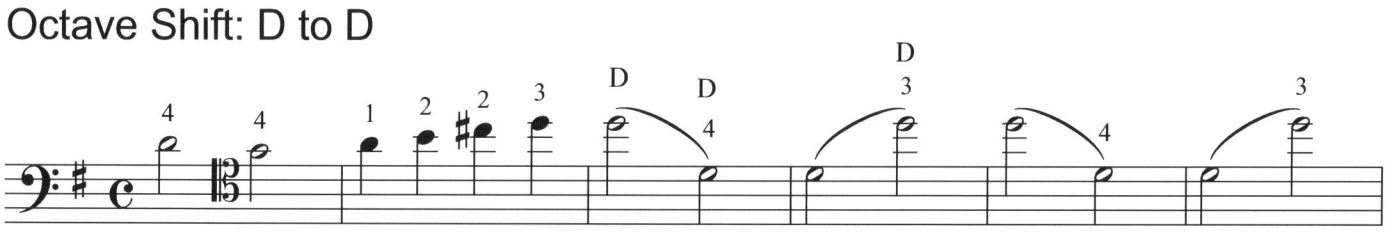
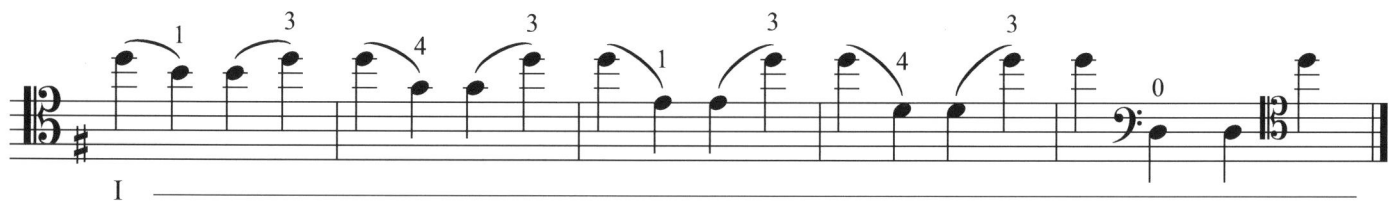

Swan Scales

Little Scales up to 8th, 7th, and 6th Positions

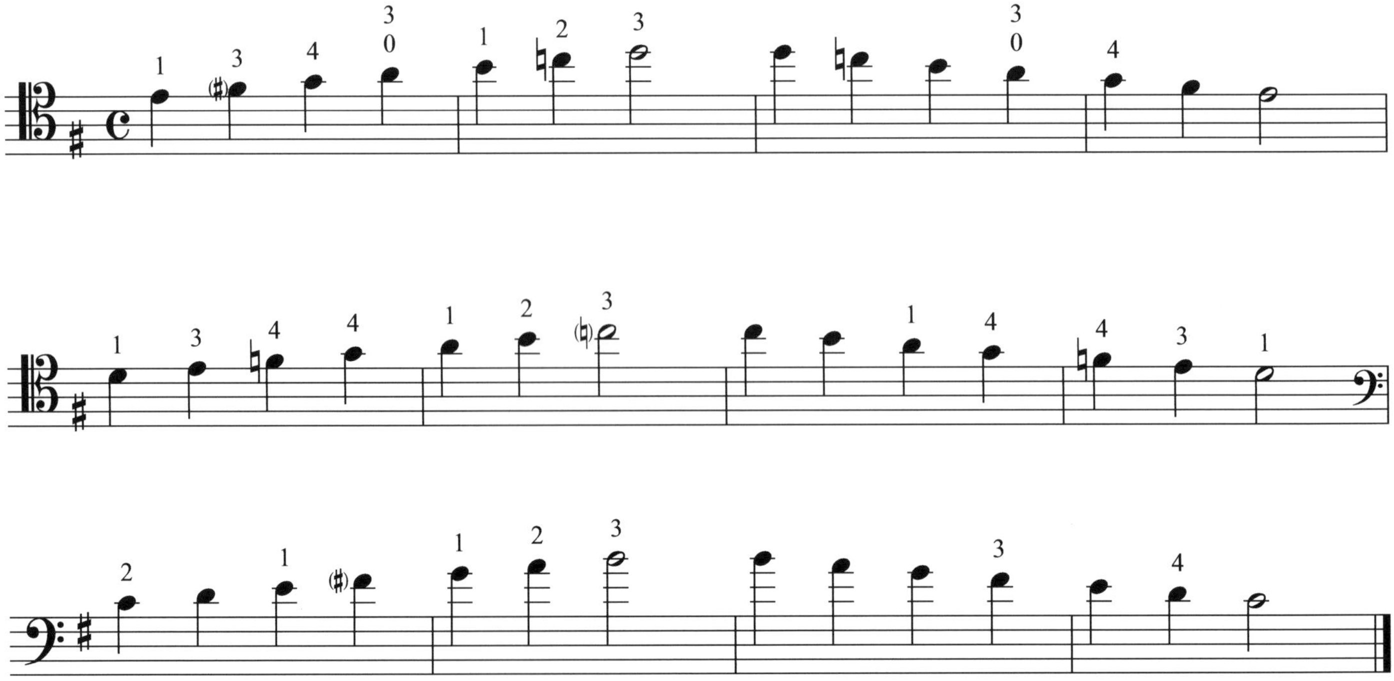

The Swan Study Book for Cello

Finger Exercise

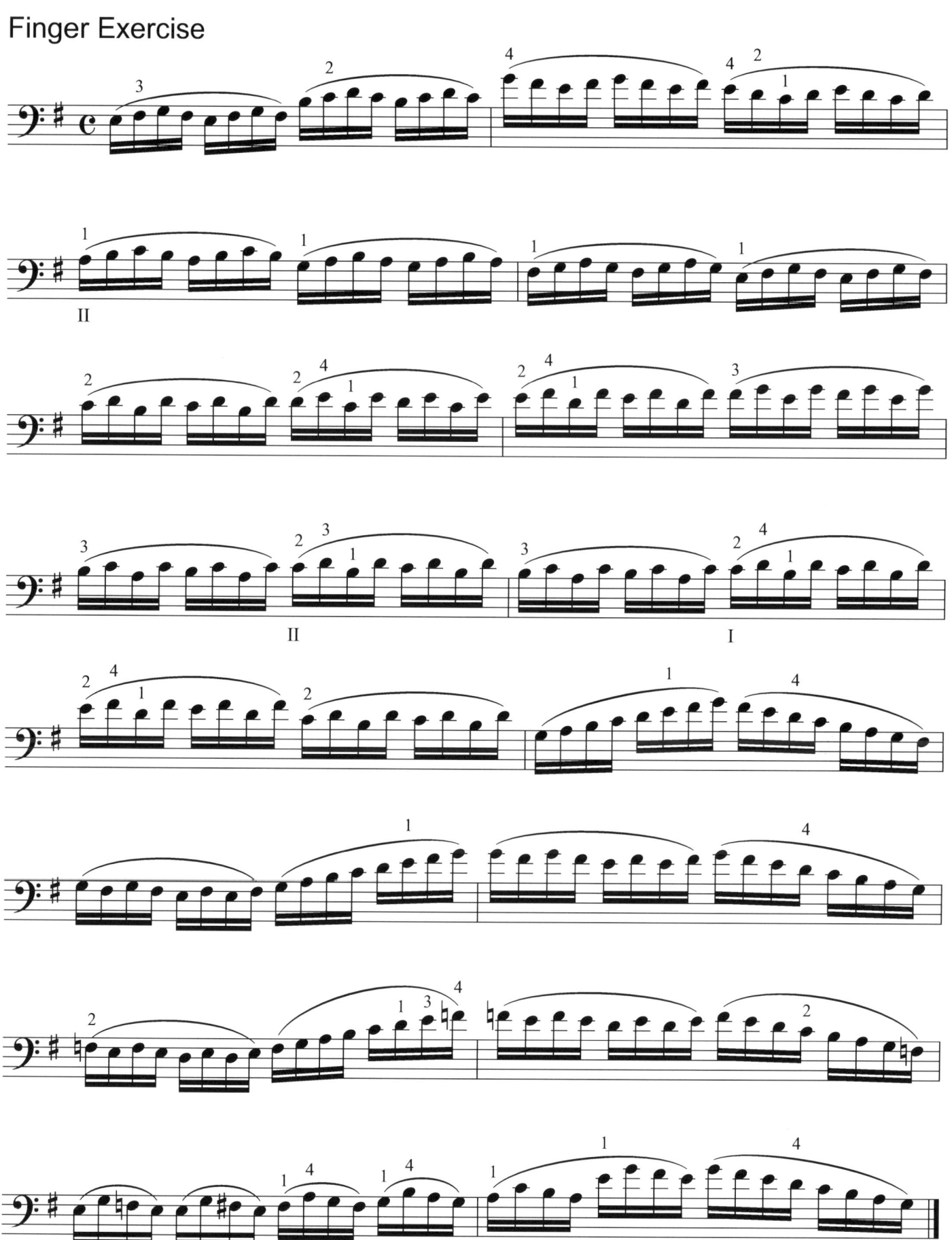

©2018 C. Harvey Publications All Rights Reserved.

The Swan Study Book for Cello

available from **www.charveypublications.com**: CHP332
The Bach Cello Suite No. 1 Study Book

Note: The Suite is broken up into sections in this study book. The complete Suite is at the back of the book.

Suite No. 1: Prelude
Part One: Measures 1-4 (Bowing #1)

Suite by J. S. Bach
Exercises by Cassia Harvey

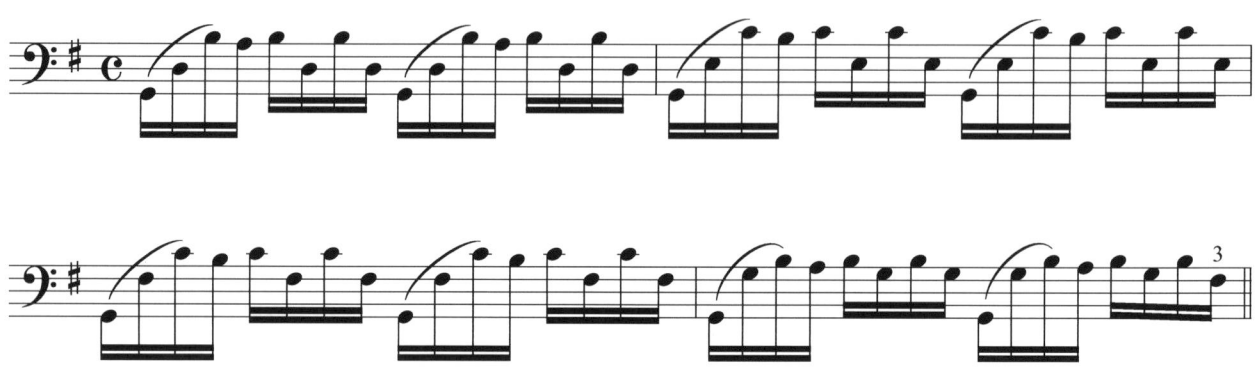

Double Stops for Intonation
Measures 1-4

©2017 C. Harvey Publications All Rights Reserved.

available from www.charveypublications.com: CHP319
The Fauré Élégie Study Book for Cello

Note: The Élégie is broken up into sections in this study book. The complete Élégie is at the back of the book.

Élégie
Part One: Measures 1-9

Élégie, Op. 24 by Gabriel Fauré
Exercises by Cassia Harvey

Key of C minor: B♭, E♭, A♭

Learning the Positions
Measures 2-5

©2017 C. Harvey Publications All Rights Reserved.

Made in the USA
San Bernardino, CA
01 July 2020